SEVEN CUPS
AND A RINGER

DAVID L. GORMAN

Seven Cups and a Ringer

Tellwell Talent
www.tellwell.ca

ISBN
978-1-77302-895-8 (Paperback)

ACKNOWLEDGEMENTS

Thanks to the interest and assistance of many, Tommy Gorman's memoirs are now available to a wider audience than found inside of a few boxes in my condo locker.

The staff at the National Archives of Canada in Ottawa made it easy for me to access the Gorman fonds in their vast files. The staff at the Hockey Hall of Fame in Toronto was most accommodating and the staff at the City of Ottawa Archives, in particular Theresa Sorel and Paul Henry have taken an interest in this project and that institution will be the permanent custodian of much of the resource material, thus ensuring its safekeeping.

Cyril Leeder, former President of the modern-day Ottawa Senators and Brian McFarlane, one of Canada's most prolific and knowledgeable hockey writers, lent their encouragement. Many friends and relatives urged me to get on with it, particularly my brother-in-law Kris Birchard who really enjoys and understands the game of hockey.

A good editor is a necessity and fortunately a long-time friend and mostly-retired university professor Tom Mcilwraith cheerfully undertook the tedious job of checking spelling, punctuation, consistency and the myriad details which make a book readable. Donna Cameron-Carter and her daughter Hadley had early looks at the manuscript and made several helpful suggestions. My son-in-law, Ed Lovekin, thankfully rescued the completed manuscript from cyberspace.

Frank Gorman(1913-1982), Tommy's son and my father, had arranged some of the material in a more cohesive manner than he found it. Father Time prevented him from completing the project but his work made it much easier to advance to the next stage.

Finally, if Thomas Patrick Gorman himself had not taken the time to chronicle the highlights of his adventurous life his descendants would be the poorer for not knowing much about the life of one of Canada's most esteemed sportsmen. Big Tommy, you had a great ride. Thanks for telling us about it.

David L. Gorman
Mississauga, 2017

TABLE OF CONTENTS

INTRODUCTION

Gowran is a pretty little town just east of Kilkenny City in the Republic of Ireland. Fewer than 1,000 souls live there in 2017, but ironically Gowran boasts one of the finest thoroughbred race tracks in all of Ireland. Ironic, because one of its descendants, Thomas Patrick (T.P.) Gorman, my grandfather, was destined to become one of North America's major players in the world of horse racing, and in so many other sporting and entertainment adventures, ice hockey in particular.

Thousands of thoroughbred racing fans descend upon Gowran today for the major racing fixtures which take place occasionally over the course of a year. Those races attract some of Europe's finest runners, wealthiest owners and greatest riders and trainers. Money, excitement, fame, fine dining, heavy betting: that is Gowran today on race day.

Two centuries ago, however, Gowran was a desperate little place. It was about that time that the Irish began leaving the Emerald Isle in search of a better, more prosperous life. The great potato famine had not yet hit. It would be the mid- 1840s before it did, but it was a hardscrabble existence for the folks around Gowran and other Irish towns even before that. No racetrack, no money, little food, few jobs. There was little reason to stay.

Thomas Gorman, T.P.'s grandfather (and my great-great grandfather), did not stay. How he got to the New World is unknown, but he was a young man when he made the decision to try his luck abroad. Born in Gowran about 1796, T.P.'s grandfather probably was no more than 25 years old when he arrived on Prince Edward Island about 1820, likely finding work in the shipyards which abounded on the Island at the time. For certain he was there in 1825, his name appearing in the Prince Edward Island *Gazette* of January 8th that year.

T.P.'s grandfather was typical of the hard-working immigrant population which had begun to arrive in Canada. He settled on Lot 13 in northwestern PEI, on the north side of the Trout River, built himself a house and set about working in the shipyards, and on his farm. By 1835 he had turned his house into Tom Gorman's Store and later he taught school, and was elected to the House of Assembly of Prince Edward Island, serving from 1839 to 1842.

By 1834 T.P.'s grandfather had married Ann Donahue, described as a petite, vivacious, pretty girl about twenty years younger than he was. That would make her a teenager, probably, when she married Tom. Ann, the daughter of immigrant parents, arrived on the Island when she was about nine. They were active, civic-minded people who, despite being Catholics in a very Protestant part of the world, were well-liked and respected in the Trout River community. Ann was, among other things, a midwife, and she helped to deliver many of the children in the community, and subsequently she taught many of the kids she had helped bring into the world.

So there the Gormans were, working in the shipyards, farming, practicing midwifery, teaching school, running a store, T.P.'s grandfather was a member of the House of Assembly, and, on top of all that, he and Ann were parents to thirteen children! Only ten survived, infant mortality being very high in those days, but the thought of even ten kids romping around would be incomprehensible to to-day's young working parents. Of course, Tom and Ann did not have to drive those kids to hockey practice every day!

Among those ten living children was another Thomas Gorman, T.P.'s father, born in 1855. He, too, was no slouch. Following the death of the patriarch in 1874, T.P.'s father, only 19 years old, gained control of the *Summerside Progress* and was its editor for a couple of years. He moved to Toronto as a reporter for *The Mail*, then to Montreal to become editor-in-chief of *The Montreal Herald*, and finally he became editor of *The Ottawa Free Press*. He was also the President of the Parliamentary Press Gallery for a time – a newspaperman to the bone.

In 1879 T.P.'s father married Mary Catherine – "Mary Kate" – MacDonald and they quickly had five children, among them one Thomas Patrick Gorman, the subject of my story. "T.P." (or "Tay Pay" to his francophone associates, and "Tommy" or "Big Tommy" to his grandchildren) hit the ground running on June 9, 1886, with newspaper blood and an entrepreneurial spirit coursing in his veins. Alas, T.P.'s father died in 1894, at less than 40 years of age, when the boy was only 8, thus depriving him of the wisdom of one of the outstanding journalists of that era.

For T.P., sitting still was never an option. This rambunctious Canadian with the strong Irish bloodlines would never understand today's bland working world. Why not take a chance? Why not have some fun? He did, in spades: page boy, Olympic gold medal winner, newspaperman, hockey icon, horse racing executive, skating show promoter, baseball team owner, arena owner and manager, race track owner, wrestling promoter. Sometimes well-off, sometimes broke, through it all T.P. displayed a zest for life that few today would have the stomach for. He lived in tumultuous times, an era which included two world wars, a depression, the birth of flight, the coming of the automobile, the arrival of television and so much more. He relished it all!

This, then, is the story of my grandfather, Thomas Patrick Gorman. Before he died, on May 15, 1961 at the age of 75, T.P. had started working on his memoirs, chronicling his amazing life full of adventure, fun, frustration and chicanery; it was never dull. Most of the material contained herein has been gathering dust in various family basements and storerooms for many years. It is now, deservedly, seeing the light of day. What follows are the words of one of Canada's most colourful and respected sporting personalities. T.P.'s story will be of interest to many, providing insight into a man who enjoyed a great ride and who contributed much to the sporting lore of this country. It is a story worth preserving.

WITH LAURIER ON THE HILL

The Gormans lived on Euclid Avenue in Ottawa South at the turn of the century and money was scarce. Thomas the father, through his journalistic work, had become friends with Sir Wilfrid Laurier, Prime Minister of Canada, but Thomas died in 1894 at the age of 38. Extra income was needed to keep the family afloat. Mary Catherine, young Tom's mom, wrote a letter to the Prime Minister and the result was a job for Tom in the House of Commons as a Page Boy. Tommy writes:

> *A day that stands out vividly in memory lane was my first as Page Boy in the House of Commons. Sir Wilfrid Laurier, the greatest of all Liberal leaders, replied to my mother's letter, requesting that I report for duty to Mr. Claire Hugg, then Chief Page. Thoughtful Sir Wilfrid also added that he would see that I was well cared for. It seems only a short time ago since my mother escorted me up to the House of Commons. She carried a little pair of brightly shined shoes and explained that she would slip them on for me. Unfortunately, as someone*

> *called my name, another pushed mother aside, grabbed my shoes and hustled me along with eight or 10 other youngsters. … It proved a thrill. … I was a small, white headed gaffer and when I reached home after my first day out in the cruel world my pockets were filled with silver which Members of Parliament had given me. That was my start.*

The year was 1895. Tommy was nine years old!

Tommy was a great admirer of Sir Wilfrid. He writes:

> *Throughout my career in the House of Commons and then in the Press Gallery Sir Wilfrid gave me some fatherly advice, which I have never forgotten. One day, Sir Wilfrid stepped quietly into his office, where I was washing blood off my battered nose and face. I hadn't anticipated his arrival or I would have tried elsewhere to remove the evidence of my latest fistic defeat. "Try to grow up to be a man of peace" Sir Wilfrid advised me with a fatherly smile. "You must keep out of trouble."*

> *Heavens! A man of peace! Every time I've moved it seems I've heard the hissing of fire engines and the rattle of tin cans. I must have been born in a thunderstorm! Even after I had left the Parliament Buildings to go into newspaper work I used to slip up to spend a precious few minutes with the most brilliant of all Canadian orators. His wonderful smile and soft, kindly voice could never be forgotten.*

As a page boy Tommy was always close to Sir Wilfrid. He recalls one sad day when

> *his private secretary called me into Sir Wilfrid's office and as I entered I could see the Prime Minister with a sad, unusual expression on his thin countenance, reading a telegram. I could sense that Sir Wilfrid had received some kind of a shock. "Tell Sir Frederick Borden to come here at once," he requested. Five minutes later I stood silently near as Sir Wilfrid, surrounded by his honourable colleagues, placed an arm around his Minister of Militia and read the contents of the telegram. I was too young then to realize the impact of the tragedy but it did strike home when Sir Frederick suddenly slumped in Sir Wilfrid's chair, covering his face with his hands. As I left the room I looked back and I could see Sir Wilfrid, with tears in his own great eyes. He then returned quietly to the Chamber where, amidst a crushing silence he announced that Sir Frederick Borden's only son had been killed in action in South Africa.*[1]

The House often sat late into the evening. Ottawa at the turn of the century was a small town and for a little guy at night, pretty scary. As he recalls,

> *trolley cars in Ottawa only operated until 10 o'clock at night. Bank Street was paved as far as Laurier Avenue and the lights disappeared at Gladstone. Hence it was dreadfully dark out to Sunnyside. I would hit the 'devil strip' between the streetcar tracks at McLeod Street and*

1 Lieut. Harold Lothrop Borden, son of Sir Frederick William Borden (1847-1917), was killed in the Second Boer War at Midrand, South Africa, on July 16, 1900. He was 24 years of age.

> *I used to sprint all the way home. Maybe that was how I developed speed.*

Enter the Dominion Policemen. They frequently accompanied the young page boy home.

> *I always felt quite safe when those blue-coated, spike-helmeted officers were around. I may have been a little nuisance to the Dominion police officers but they had received instructions to look after me and they never failed to do so.*

But you can't remain a page boy forever, so, Tommy headed off to the newspaper world, a career which, given his family's background, he came by honestly.

Page Boys hockey team c. 1910

> **P***eople have often asked, 'How did you become a newspaper writer?' Well, after starting life as a page boy in the House of Commons I transferred several years later to the Parliamentary Press Gallery. Between sessions I delivered papers, ran messages, looked after*

> *furnaces and incidentally played lacrosse, hockey and football. I was really an active little man.*
>
> *One day Robert McLeod, beloved Ottawa correspondent for Reuters, offered sympathetically to try and land me a job with the Citizen Company. He took me down and introduced me to Harry S. Southam. "He's pretty young, Robert," Mr. Southam said, looking me over with a kind pair of bright eyes. "What could he do?"*
>
> *"Not very much of anything" explained Mr. McLeod "but he is willing to learn." And that was my break into the newspaper atmosphere. I think I did nearly everything around the Citizen. D'Arcy Finn declared that I was the worst furnace man they ever had and Dave Reynolds always rated me as a terrible proof reader. I studied hard however to learn shorthand and typewriting, and became pretty good at both.*

He became pretty good as a reporter too. In 1911 he overheard Fred 'Cyclone' Taylor declare that he would score a goal while skating backwards. Tommy reported that now-famous story, and was instantly promoted to Sports Editor of the *Citizen*. That was a pretty lofty perch for a 25-year-old.

> *In 1912 I was in New York on a visit when the Titanic crashed an iceberg in the Atlantic. From the Cunard Line dock, amid tears and tragedy I told the story of the survivors.*

He was at the *Citizen* through the war years when along came an unforgettable event for Canada, the awful Halifax explosion in December, 1917, when two ships , one loaded with munitions, collided in Halifax harbor. The resulting explosion killed or injured thousands. Tommy was quickly on his way to cover the event for the *Citizen*.

> *After I had scooped nearly every paper in North America, H.S. Southam wired me 'Congratulations to Canada's Number One Reporter'. That made me feel pretty good, though the message was delivered in the Halifax Military Jail where they had taken me because I had violated some of their censorship regulations. They released me with a warning. I have since been in better jails than that at Halifax! The commanding officer however complimented me. He referred to me as a 'journalist'. Such flattery!*

A SMASHED-UP FACE AND A GOLD MEDAL

More than one hundred years ago lacrosse was Canada's national game, a rough-and-tumble sport played by a hardy few and watched by thousands. T.P. was among the former.

> *Back in the glorious days of the National Lacrosse Union, lacrosse was really strenuous. I played my first intermediate lacrosse for Ottawa Nationals at Quebec one Sunday afternoon. In the second quarter someone hit me from behind for six stitches. I thought the grandstand had fallen on me. My professional debut took place at New Westminster as a member of the Regina Capitals, Minto Cup challengers. There were 15 thousand people in the stands and around the field. In the second period Tom Gifford hit me so hard he broke my jaw, cracked my nose and knocked out four front teeth. I woke up in one of the Vancouver hospitals. Someone was moaning loudly in the next room. "Who*

is that?" I asked, "and what is that moaning? "Quiet, please," said my teammate. "That's the guy who hit you."

Tommy in his lacrosse uniform

That hit ended Gorman's lacrosse career. But he loved to tell stories about his time in the game. Here is one of them.

Besides being a marvelous hockey player, Fred 'Cyclone' Taylor also became a first class lacrosse fielder. The Listowel terror could run all day. For their games against Shamrocks at the old Mile Ends grounds in Montreal, the Ottawa Capitals used to take a special rail car and diner, which they would park a few hundred yards from the Shamrock field. They would dine and dress on the

Pullman[2] and then run over to the playing grounds. One Saturday afternoon, with just two minutes to go, groundskeepers opened all the gates, so that there would not be too much congestion when eight or 10,000 people rushed toward the exits.

Johnnie Howard and Jim Kavanagh had 'Cyclone' cornered and were laying on the hickory pretty heavily as Taylor ran back and forth in a plucky effort to escape the giant defencemen of the famous Shamrock team. Kavanagh and Howard were closing in for the kill when Taylor suddenly spied an open gate behind him. Out he went, ball and all, running all the way to the Capital special. Referees of course stopped the game and gave Taylor a penalty, though they could not specify what it was for. Play ended without further scoring and Taylor's team mates found him quite cheerful and comfortable when they reached their Pullman. "I fooled the Shamrocks that time," commented the celebrated Cyclone. He did, too, though he had an assist on his unexpected escape ... from the groundskeepers!

And he enjoys telling this story about his days in London, and his Olympic gold medal. It was October 24, 1908 at White City in London, England and young Tommy, an energetic 22 year-old was playing for the Canadian Olympic Lacrosse Team. He was the youngest member of that team. A total of 18 nations participated in that, the fourth

2 'Pullman' was the popular way of describing the railroad sleeping car, owned by the Pullman Company of Chicago and carried on regular passenger trains. Lacrosse and hockey teams were heavy users of Pullman cars for travelling overnight between cities.

Olympiad, an event widely credited with resurrecting the flagging Olympic movement.

> *In 1908 they selected me to represent Ottawa on the Canadian Olympic Lacrosse team. We defeated All England at the White City stadium and I had the honour of scoring the first goal. That British team however gave us a stubborn battle. The late King George V, then Prince of Wales, presented the Olympic Gold Medals and it was a proud moment. That Olympic Gold Medal naturally was among my most prized possessions. However, I was very young at the time and I seemed to get in continuous hot water with Manager William Foran and Coach Jimmie Murphy.*
>
> *Two or three times I became lost in the London fog and once, Joe Lalley threatened to send me home 'on the next boat.' We had one very hard-fought game against the North of England … and everything appeared to break right for me. I scored three fast goals in the first period and two more in the second, after which Messrs. Foran, Murphy and Lalley came around to assure me I could remain with the Olympic team, providing I would agree 1) to keep out of the Irish Village at White City; 2) not to use rough language toward my aristocratic and distinguished-looking English opponents; 3) to stay away from Piccadilly Circus and Hyde Park; and 4) not to go diving or swimming any more in my lacrosse uniform.*
>
> *It made me somewhat embarrassed but very proud when likeable William Foran patted me, the youngest player on the team, and said: "You are a great lacrosse*

player." Still, I often recall that my fellow employees at the Citizen had to pass around the hat before I left for England. If they had not done so I could not have gone because I was a real amateur.

I recently experienced great delight in saying to Barbara Ann Scott: 'Don't be so ritzy, Barb. I'm an Olympic champion too!'

T.P.'s Gold Medal, and the Canadian team, Tommy on the right.

Today, in 2017, Toronto basketball fans have turned a few thousand square feet of concrete outside the Air Canada Centre into what is fondly known as Jurassic Park. It is where large crowds gather to watch their sneaker-squeaking Raptors perform on the huge TV screen facing the square. It is a lot of fun. But while such gatherings, using modern technology are indeed fun, the concept is hardly new. It existed more than 100 years ago, without the technology of course, but fun with a capital F just the same. Tommy recalls:

In the prosperous old days when lacrosse boomed from coast to coast, railroad excursions were the popular fad. Over the New York and Ottawa railway, the Ottawa

> *Capitals used to organize low-priced runs for their games at Cornwall. Trains would pull out of Central Station at 1:15 p.m. and hundreds of civil servants, leaving their offices on Parliament Hill, would rush down Wellington Street in time to pile into the special coaches. Sometimes, the Capitals would be accompanied to Cornwall by 11 or 12 hundred rooters. They would take along their own brass band and of course there would be a parade from the Cornwall station to the East End grounds. After each game, there would be another procession, win or lose, back to the depot. Shamrocks and Nationals also operated excursions from Montreal to Ottawa and the Irish would invade Ottawa several hundred strong. They too would have their band and the Montrealers would march ahead of their lacrosse club bus, right to Varsity Oval. If the Shamrocks won they would rush out on the field to carry their heroes off shoulder high. When the National Lacrosse Union folded they closed the book on one of Canada's most fascinating sports chapters.*

An Olympic Gold Medal in London started it. A smashed-up face in Vancouver ended it. It was just another chapter in a remarkable life.

1905: THE START OF AN AMAZING HOCKEY CAREER

Before he was 20 years of age Tommy had seen very little hockey. It was an interesting time in the development of North America, with Oklahoma and New Mexico joining the United States in 1905, and a new car, still regarded as a toy by most people, costing about $1,500 or about twice the average annual income. You could buy a loaf of bread for .04 cents and the miracle of flight was just beginning to take shape. Orville and Wilbur Wright logged their longest flight so far, a 38 minute, three second jaunt.

Young Tom saw his first important hockey game that year, at the old Dey's Gladstone Avenue arena in Ottawa. It was a contest between the famed Silver Seven (Ottawa Senators) and the Montreal Victorias.

> *Billy Smith and I were playing on the canal under the Bank Street Bridge when Alf Smith, Billy's brother, came along and shouted down "If you kids go home and get dressed and cleaned, I will take you to the hockey match." Did we hustle. Through a little side door at*

> *the arena the greatest right wing for his size that the game has ever produced slipped us through, saying we could find seats in the rush end. We did that in a hurry. Spectators stood four and five deep in the old arena. Suddenly a roar went up and there came a clattering of skates on the wooden stairway as the incomparable Senators signaled their initial appearance. Down they came and through the little gate they stepped out. Harvey Pulford, Art Moore, Harry Westwick, Alf Smith, Billy Gilmour. Several thousand fans cheered wildly and then set up a maddening cry: "McGee, McGee, we want McGee!" They eagerly stretched their necks to see their idol, Frank McGee, the most brilliant center ice player in hockey. And McGee carried out his entry with true dramatic sportsmanship, skating over the frozen surface as the Ottawa supporters went wild. His white pants had been pressed to a knife-like edge; his blonde hair he had parted and combed to perfection; his boots had been shined and his new stick brightly taped. McGee held his stick in spotless white gloves and slowly skated down to join his teammates.*

Frank McGee was one of the greatest hockey players of that era and his entrance obviously resonated with Tommy, sitting in the rush end awaiting the start of his first important hockey game. He took it all in.

> *They faced off at center ice and McGee proceeded to steal the show. Three times he seized the puck near his own defence, plunged at blinding speed through the Victoria team to drive a deadly shot into the Montreal nets and after each goal he would glide quickly back*

to his own position and bend over his stick, eager and ready to go again.

Tommy describes some of McGee's great on-ice performances.

Frank scored 12 goals in a game against the Dawson City Nuggets, he saved the Stanley Cup in a play-off series against Wanderers, and until he retired at the height of his career the inimitable McGee stood head and shoulders over every other Canadian forward. The blonde hockey demon attained this supremacy in the days of natural ice, short schedules and thirty-minute periods during all of which he played without relief. They say he had the sight of only one eye when he played for Ottawa, though I always doubted it. Nevertheless he was, without doubt, the greatest and most spectacular center man that hockey has ever produced. In modern hockey with his terrific speed, clever stick-handling and grim, merciless determination Frank McGee would still have been supreme.

Tommy recalls clearly another day, this time in 1915 after McGee had volunteered for duty overseas during World War 1.

One afternoon, bands played on Parliament Hill and khaki-clad regiments marched through excited throngs fearlessly towards Union Station to entrain for Great Britain. "There's Frank McGee" we heard several say as he swung proudly ahead of his little company. On this occasion there were no shouts for Frank McGee. Instead there were sighs and tear-dimmed eyes, sad farewells and silent prayers. Overseas casualty lists soon began to come in, there were many heart-broken

> *homes in Ottawa and elsewhere throughout Canada and one night the 'Killed In Action' list contained the name of Lieut. Frank McGee. He had been shot down while leading a raiding platoon out of the British trenches in France. Soldiers found him the next afternoon and buried him in a peaceful little French cemetery behind the firing lines, the greatest of all center ice puck chasers.*

By then Tommy was no longer a youngster. He was almost 30 when McGee died, and into his early 30s when World War 1 ended. That amazing night in 1905, as a 19 year-old in Dey's Arena stuck with him. Hockey was to become his passion for the next 40-plus years. But he wasn't one-dimensional. Horse racing was also a passion, and all kinds of rollicking adventures in the often wacky world of sports and entertainment consumed him for the rest of his life.

ON TO THE BIG TIME

How did T.P. Gorman get into big-time hockey? With not much money, a little luck, and a benefactor.

> *Many indeed were the conflicting stories as to how I had originally broken into professional hockey. This is the true version. In 1917, just before the formation of the National Hockey League, the old Ottawa Hockey Association decided to toss in the sponge. Their franchise, club and players were for sale for $5,000. George Kendall, whose press representative I had been in Ottawa at $10 per week, telephoned from Montreal and inquired "Why don't you buy that Ottawa team? You could make it go. They want only five grand!"*
>
> *"George" I explained apologetically, "I couldn't buy it if they just needed $500." "Well, you are not a bad guy," continued Kendall. "Come on down, we'll see what we can do." George quickly advanced me $2,500 and with 'Ted' Dey we bought the Ottawa Hockey Association.*

> *Hockey boomed wildly in Ottawa following the war and in January, 1925, I sold out to Frank Ahearn for $35,000 and his shares in the Connaught Park Jockey Club. Had it not been for the likeable George Kendall, however, I might never have gone into hockey. I paid George back out of our first year's profits. Only on one occasion was the Canadien owner really angry. He wanted a goalkeeper and I assigned him Sammy Goderre. Two weeks later Kendall shouted over the 'phone "Send down and get this guy out of my training camp. He is a poker player, not a goalkeeper, and he has all our other men broke!"*

T.P's Senators quickly won three Stanley Cups, beating Seattle in Toronto in 1920, Vancouver on the west coast in 1921, and Edmonton in Vancouver in 1923.

> *I always wanted to win the Stanley Cup in my own home town, Ottawa, but was never able to do so. Toronto St. Pats beat out the Senators in 1922 and the Canadiens repeated in 1924. That was my last season with the Senators in the NHL.*

It was the 1923 team that provided T.P. with his biggest thrill in hockey. Writing in Ottawa's French-language newspaper *Le Droit* in 1937, Tommy recalls:

> *My greatest thrill came when Ottawa won the World's Championship and the Stanley Cup from the Edmonton Eskimos at Vancouver in April, 1923. It was a big thrill to win the Stanley Cup with the Chicago Black Hawks in 1934 and another to land the trophy again in 1935 with the Montreal Maroons, but somehow that game*

in Vancouver and Harry Broadbent's winning goal stands out vividly. It is doubtful if ever a team carried on under such adverse conditions and went through so many trials to triumph as did the Senators in 1923. Sprague Cleghorn had gone to Canadiens to add a fighting punch to the Habitants and Ottawa had broken in two youngsters whose names were destined to become famous-Frank Clancy and Lionel Hitchman. Canadiens and Ottawa met in the finals and after a hectic series, during which Sprague Cleghorn and Billy Coutu drew suspensions for cutting down Lionel Hitchman and Cy Denneny respectively, the Senators carried off the eastern championship and again set out for Vancouver.

Denneny and Hitchman boarded the Imperial Limited with their heads swathed in bandages. The Ottawa team had been badly crippled in the eastern play-offs and none of the hockey critics conceded Ottawa any chance of bringing back the Cup. We only had about eight solid players left and were faced with the terrific task of defeating both the Vancouver Millionaires and the Edmonton Eskimos.

Ottawa immediately astounded the hockey world by outscoring Vancouver in the first game of the series. Stepping off the train and onto the ice without an hour's rest they vanquished the highly-touted Vancouver team. Three nights later the Senators defeated Vancouver again, earning the right to oppose Edmonton in two out of three for the Stanley Cup. What chance, asked the critics, would Ottawa have against this wonderfully fast Edmonton club? Edmonton led in the first game by 1-0 until a few minutes before the finish when Lionel Hitchman rushed from end to end and whipped in a shot to tie it. Then came the overtime. The western fans expected Ottawa to assume defensive tactics but again the Senators out-guessed the Eskimos. They launched a withering attack and in less than two minutes Cy Denenny had punched home the winning goal.

Two nights later Ottawa faced Edmonton again. They afterwards told us that thousands of lights burned bright in Ottawa that night and that hundreds actually prayed for the success of their battle-scarred heroes who had journeyed 3,000 miles to fight for Ottawa's hockey honours. Eddie Gerard and Buck Boucher had been injured; little Harry Helman lay in the Vancouver hospital with his face painfully cut. Only six players remained intact…and what a game it was!

Frank Clancy actually played every position on the Ottawa team that night. He even went into the nets when Clint Benedict drew a penalty in the last 10 minutes. Eddie Gerard actually fought his way out of my arms to replace the fallen Hitchman and Frank Nighbor played the entire 60 minutes without a rest. Harry Broadbent's winning goal was fired in the first period, a rising shot from the right boards catching the upper left side of the Edmonton net. It was a hockey shot that rang out around the hockey world and though the fast-skating Eskimos, urged on by 5,000 howling maniacs from the Prairies fought with desperation to tie it up they could not do so and the bell rang with the Ottawas champions of the world and again holders of the Stanley Cup. I will always maintain that this was not only my greatest thrill, but that it was Ottawa's most outstanding achievement in any form of sport.

The homecoming of the new World's Champions proved a magnificent one! If the Ottawa hockey fans had shouted in 1921 they cheered themselves hoarse in 1923. Automobile parades, banquets, theatre parties, dinners, a civic reception, gold watches, all the reward for a magnificent display of grit and skill.

the Ottawa Senators. c.1920 with T.P. second from the right, back row.

AMBROSE O'BRIEN AND THE NATIONAL HOCKEY ASSOCIATION

That 1905 Silver Sevens game was the genesis of Tommy's interest in hockey, and the fateful telephone call from George Kendall in 1917 initiated his first financial foray into the sport. As the Sports Editor of the *Ottawa Citizen* for some of those intervening years, T.P. had become acutely aware of the off-ice developments which eventually led to the formation of the National Hockey League.

Ottawa and the surrounding area became known far and wide as "The Cradle of Hockey" and with good reason. Towering business people such as J. Ambrose O'Brien,[3] Frank Ahearn[4] and J.R. Booth[5] began to take an interest in the sport and Tommy had a ring-side seat for some of the developments.

Here is how Tommy remembers those early days:

---

3 John Ambrose O'Brien (1885-1968) was an industrialist from Renfrew, Ontario.

4 Frank Ahearn (1886-1962) was an Ottawa businessman and Member of Parliament

5 John Rudolphus Booth (1827-1925) was a major figure in the Ottawa valley timber industry in the 19th century. He owned timber limits in Algonquin Park, financed the railway between Georgian Bay and New England, and built mills in Aylmer and Hull.

Away back in the summer of 1909 several Renfrew citizens, including Messrs. J.G. Barnet[6] *and Hon. Thomas Low*[7] *decided that Renfrew should be represented in Big Time hockey. At that time the Ottawa Hockey Club was competing in a shaky organization known as The Eastern League. It consisted of Ottawa, Quebec and Shamrocks. Messrs. Barnet and Low approached youthful Ambrose O'Brien, who had played for several seasons on the Renfrew club. They had won all the available honours in the Ottawa Valley League and had become highly ambitious. Mr. O'Brien consented to see what could be done on behalf of his home town and he made written application to the Eastern League. That application was refused, as was that of the Montreal Wanderers, then represented by Jimmie Strachan*[8] *and Bill Jennings.*[9]

"Why don't we organize a new league, Ambrose?" Jimmie Strachan asked. "I know their group is shaky." And that was actually the inception of the National Hockey Association, the predecessor to the National Hockey League.

Within a few days O'Brien had launched Les Canadiens and had them housed in the old Montagnard Rink in north-east Montreal. The Renfrew club was admitted

6 J.G. Barnet was president of the Renfrew Millionaires hockey club in 1910.

7 Thomas A. Low (1871-1931) was a Quebec industrialist and lumberman and Member of Parliament.

8 Jimmie Strachan (1876-1939) was a Montreal ice hockey executive and businessman.

9 Bill Jennings was a vice-president with the Montreal Wanderers.

and Mr. O'Brien had also arranged, with the assistance of his father Senator M.J. O'Brien[10], to include Cobalt and Haileybury. Shamrocks, then represented by one of the greatest hockey players of all-time, Harry Trihey, suddenly decided to withdraw from the Eastern League and the Quebec Bull-dogs followed suit. This left the Ottawa and All-Montreal clubs in desperate circumstances though the Senators had a formidable club. Owner Wally Bate[11] and his confrères realized that the Eastern League was doomed and it was decided to jump, if possible, to the National Hockey Association.

During a meeting of the new organization in Montreal, presided over by Ambrose O'Brien, the Ottawa Senators were admitted, sounding the death knell of the Eastern League and consolidating the National Hockey Association with six clubs: the Montreal Wanderers, Les Canadiens, Cobalt, Haileybury, Renfrew and Ottawa.

Ambrose O'Brien at one time financed and controlled four of the NHA clubs. All the games were desperately fought and there was never a suspicion of dishonest competition, though gambling continued furiously, particularly in the Silver country. Jack Laviolette was the first coach signed by Mr. O'Brien for Les Canadiens and Joe Cattarinich started out in goal. Other famous

---

10 Michael John O'Brien (1851-1940), a Nova Scotian who moved to Renfrew in 1879, was a railway builder, industrialist and philanthropist. He established a silver mine in Cobalt, Ontario in 1903, and was a Senator for Ontario from 1918 to 1925. He donated the O'Brien Cup to the NHA league; it was used until 1950 by the National Hockey League and is in the collection of the Hockey Hall of Fame.

11 Wally Bate was Llewellyn Bate, an important figure in Ottawa's early hockey days.

players in Montreal included 'Newsy' Lalonde and Didier Pitre. Renfrew imported Lester Patrick, Frank Patrick and after a sensational "raid" they captured Fred 'Cyclone' Taylor from Ottawa. They were known as the Renfrew Millionaires and they provided terrific advertising for Renfrew.

The Millionaires made a terrific championship bid in 1910 but lost out to the powerful Montreal Wanderers, whose personnel then included the likes of Riley Hern and other top stars. By this time the Pacific Coast League had started making fantastic offers to the stars of the NHA. Mr. O'Brien transferred the Haileybury franchise to Charlie Querrie[12]*, who launched the Toronto club and, having decided to withdraw himself sought a purchaser for Les Canadiens in Montreal.*

O'Brien eventually found one in the person of George Kennedy[13] who soon became recognized as one of the smartest promoters in hockey. He handled the team until his death in 1921, after which the club passed into the hands of Joe Cattarinich,[14] Leo Dandurand[15] and Louis Letourneau.[16] They held it until 1938, when it was purchased by the Canadian Arena Company.

---

12 Charles L. Querrie (1877-1950) of Markham, Ontario, was General Manager of the Toronto Arenas hockey club from 1917 to 1920.

13 George Washington Kendall (1881-1921), known as George Kennedy, of Montreal; wrestler.

14 Joseph Jean Etienne Stanislas 'Joe' Cattarinich (1881-1938), of Quebec City.

15 Joseph Viateur 'Leo' Dandurand (1889-1964), from Illinois, who moved to Canada about 1905.

16 Louis A. Letourneau (1868-1952).

> *Hockey has come a long way since Ambrose O'Brien and the Renfrew Millionaires pioneered the NHA. It is said that Mr. O'Brien disposed of his interest in Les Canadiens to George Kennedy for $2,500 and it is known that Joe Cattarinich, Leo Dandurand and Louis Letourneau took over Les Habitants for $11,000, after which they sold out to the Canadian Arena Company 19 years later for $165,000.*

"What price Les Canadiens now?" wondered T.P. in 1957 as he writes in his memoirs. He would be astonished, absolutely dumbfounded, to know that by 2016, *Forbes Magazine* valued the Montreal Canadiens at almost $1.2 billion! In the same year Las Vegas interests paid a staggering $500 million, just to join the National Hockey League.

The NHA, finally naming Frank Calder[17] as President, continued until November, 1917 when Les Canadiens, Montreal Wanderers, Ottawa, Toronto and Quebec withdrew to launch the National Hockey League.

---

17 Frank Sellick Calder (1877-1943), NHL president from 1917 to 1943. Emigrated from United Kingdom to Montreal, probably in 1890s.

THE 'PHONE CALL, A NEW LEAGUE, AND TWO WONDERFUL MEN

Tom Gorman was just 31 years of age when he received that fateful call from George Kennedy, a call which had a profound influence on the direction of Gorman's life from that point on. It launched what would become a Hall of Fame career and it was, in retrospect, the beginning of the National Hockey League.

George Kennedy wasn't always George Kennedy. He was born in Montreal in 1896 as Georges Kendall, son of a prim and proper Irish Catholic lass and a prominent Scottish Protestant Montreal businessman G.H. Kendall. Young Georges though, didn't quite fit the family mold. He became an outstanding boxer, later a wrestling promoter, and then a hockey team owner. For those apparent transgressions his well-to-do Montreal family practically disowned him. Georges had an easy answer. He simply changed his name from Georges Kendall to George Kennedy and went about his own business, in his own way.

Tommy was a fervent admirer of the Montreal sportsman regardless of the name he used. He writes:

A broad-shouldered, bright-eyed sportsman, who now lies peacefully in Côte des Neiges Cemetery contributed greatly to the formation and ultimate success of the National Hockey League. This is the late George Kennedy, original owner of Les Canadiens and one of the five men present when the National Hockey league came into existence in the fall of 1917.

When Ambrose O'Brien, after a bitter fight with the old Eastern Hockey League, sought someone to take charge of a French club in Montreal George was recommended. The National Hockey Association became a reality and Kennedy, backed by Mr. O'Brien, accepted the Canadien franchise. Les Canadiens played for two seasons in the old Montagnard Arena and then moved up to the Westmount Arena. When the latter burned down, things looked very bleak but Kennedy saved the situation by switching the team down to the old Jubilee Rink. He refused to quit and did remarkably well at the Jubilee. Kennedy signed such brilliant hockey stars as Georges Vezina, Newsy Lalonde, Didier Pitre, Joe Cattarinich, Joe Hall and Joe Malone.

In the spring of 1917 another bitter hockey fight broke out, this time between Toronto forces headed by Eddie Livingstone and Percy Quinn, and the Eastern group which consisted of Les Canadiens, Ottawa Senators and Quebec Bull-dogs. Quinn and Livingstone sought to oust Toronto St. Pats from the Mutual Street arena and to start a new circuit in which they had also reserved a franchise for Hamilton. George Kennedy proved a terrific fighter and was well backed-up by President Frank Calder. Eventually Kennedy, Calder and I, then in command at Ottawa, managed to secure the Mutual Street Arena for St. Patricks. Hamilton decided to join with the eastern group and the Quinn-Livingston combination had to admit defeat.

Shortly afterwards, George Kennedy, Frank Calder, Mike Quinn, Sam Lichtenheim and I assembled in a little room at the Windsor Hotel in Montreal, where the National Hockey League came into existence. Ottawa, Les Canadiens, and Quebec withdrew from the NHA and accepted franchises in the National Hockey League. Kennedy was the important factor in the formation of the National Hockey League as he had quietly financed operations of two of the other clubs.

The minutes of that meeting, the very first minutes of what would become one of the world's most successful sports leagues, read as follows: 'At a meeting of representatives of Hockey Clubs held at the Windsor Hotel, Montreal November 22nd, 1917, the following present: G.W. Kendall (Kennedy), S.E. Lichtenheim, T.P. Gorman, M.J. Quinn and Frank Calder it was explained by the last named that in view of the suspension of operations by the National Hockey Association of Canada Limited, he had called the meeting at the suggestion of the Quebec Hockey Club to ascertain if some steps could not be taken to perpetuate the game of Hockey.'

Frank Calder was elected to the Chair and a discussion ensued after which it was moved by T.P. Gorman, seconded by G.W. Kendall (Kennedy) 'that the Canadiens, Wanderers, Ottawa and Quebec Hockey Clubs unite to compose the National Hockey League.' The motion was carried. Those men would have had no idea at the time, but a multi-billion dollar business, the National Hockey League, was born.

The Windsor Hotel.

It was in the spring of 1919 that tragedy struck heavily at the National Hockey League. After winning the NHL title George Kennedy took Les Canadiens to Seattle for the Stanley Cup series. Unfortunately the unforgettable world-wide flu pandemic had broken out at the coast and after two games had been played civic authorities at Seattle refused to permit public gatherings, after which Les Canadiens and Seattle called off their series.

That pandemic infected a fifth of the world's population and killed as many as 40 million people, including more than 675,000 in the United States.

> *'Bad Joe' Hall was the first of George Kennedy's little squad to collapse through the flu and though everything possible was done to save him the famous Brandon star died at Seattle. Several other Canadien players fell down with the dread disease. George Kennedy appeared immune and it was he who looked after, with tireless persistence, the stricken puck-chasers from Montreal.*
>
> *However, George also contracted the flu and shortly after his return to Montreal, he collapsed. George fought one of his gamest fights but sank steadily and succumbed the following autumn, when just at the height of what would have been a wonderful career.*
>
> *If George Kennedy had survived the entire hockey future might have been changed. He was dead set against allowing any of the United States clubs in and would never have consented to the admittance of Boston, New York, Chicago, Detroit and Pittsburgh. "Those Yankee fellows have too much money for us" he used to comment. "They will build bigger rinks and steal all our star players. They will only get in over my dead body!"*

And that was what they eventually did.

> *Kennedy was a grand fellow in every respect. He loved his wife sincerely and was simply wild about his only daughter. George shopped around in every city he visited and never returned without some beautiful present for*

his only child. He spoke both French and English fluently and had also, in his trips overseas in quest of wrestlers, acquired some knowledge of European languages. When he passed away, the National Hockey League lost its most colourful director. He would have become America's number one promoter.

George Kennedy

Gorman and Kennedy in many ways were two peas in a pod. They were fun-loving, gregarious, mischievous, ambitious, practical jokers, and intensely competitive. Tommy recalls a couple of NHL meetings which he and Kennedy attended.

In the early days of the leaky-roofed NHL each club was allowed two votes. George Kennedy and Nap Duval showed up for Les Canadiens at a Montreal meeting. I had gone down from Ottawa alone. "You must have another representative" George Kennedy had warned me. "They might spring a sudden vote on us." So, with Kennedy heading the plot, I took in Raymond Cazeaux, the famous old French wrestler. 'Cazooks' was really something. Every time Frank Calder read a motion, he would jump to his feet and shout the only two English words George Kennedy had taught him: "We protest!" Finally, Frank Calder's patience was exhausted. "You take that big wrestler out of here or I will throw you out with him" he warned. "You and Kennedy are trying to make a farce out of the National Hockey League!"

Another time, George moved that I be fined $500 by the NHL for 'conduct detrimental to the interests of hockey.' This was over a voting contest among the NHL managers for most valuable player on each club. I voted for one of the goal judges for the Canadiens.

On other occasions, meetings were held in Toronto.

Ontario was then bone dry and every session in Toronto called for an after-the-meeting party. Frank Calder signed the dinner checks and George Kennedy supplied the champagne. He always carried a suitcase which had a false bottom, and he never failed to produce the wine.

It is not surprising that these two, promoters first and foremost, got along so well together. But there had been a few hiccups along the way to the birth of the NHL. There were some serious difficulties sorting out the Toronto situation, where Eddie Livingstone and Percy Quinn had their own ideas about where to take pro hockey, and there were financial issues too. T.P. remembers it this way:

Had it not been for Major John Bassett, the National Hockey League might never have been organized. In the fall of 1917, Percy Quinn and Eddie Livingstone attempted to secure complete control of the Mutual Street Arena in Toronto. This, of course was before the erection of Maple Leaf Gardens. Canadiens and Ottawa had linked up and Frank Calder had received assurances that Hamilton would swing along with Canadiens and Ottawa, providing that Percy Thompson of Hamilton could be assured that Toronto would be included.

Calder also learned that the Mutual Street Arena was heavily indebted to the Imperial Bank of Canada. Calder appeared unable to secure an appointment with the Imperial Bank manager in Toronto and it was Major Bassett who finally managed to get one. At the request of Major Bassett, Frank Calder, George Kennedy and I conferred at Toronto with the Imperial Bank representative. The correct picture was presented and they agreed to sign a contract with Charlie Querrie, Paul Ciceri and the Hambly boys, who then called their club the Toronto Arenas. This left Quinn and Livingstone out in the cold as Hamilton agreed to come into the new organization, but not to operate until the following season. And that was exactly how Toronto crashed through to the Big Time Hockey.

In its first season the National Hockey League consisted of Ottawa Senators, Toronto Arenas, Les Canadiens and Montreal Wanderers. The Wanderers withdrew following the destruction of the Westmount Arena by fire

> *in 1918 and the pro hockey circuit wound up with only three teams. The Toronto Arenas changed their name to St. Patricks and were subsequently sold to Connie Smythe and his associates, after which Smythe's dream of Maple Leaf Gardens and a colossal hockey empire became a reality.*
>
> *I often wonder however, what might have happened if Major John Bassett, then a politically powerful figure in Ottawa, had not interceded for the Ottawa-Canadien interests, with the Imperial Bank. Until Major Bassett stepped in, things looked very bleak indeed for the proposed National Hockey League, now a tremendous organization. Major Bassett was, at that time, a director of the Ottawa Hockey Association and I recall his saying over luncheon at the Rideau Club in Ottawa: "Don't worry over that Toronto situation, my good friend. I will call those Imperial Bank fellows and read the riot act to them." I have always thought that the good Major acted accordingly, because the Imperial Bank directors gave us a red carpet reception and the Toronto Arenas received a contract, which enabled them to join us at the next meeting of the new group, drinking champagne which George Kennedy had smuggled up from Montreal in the false bottom of his suitcase. That was in the good old days of prohibition.*

The next big crisis for the still-young league came in 1923. Gorman's Senators had already won the Stanley Cup twice, and were doing well.

> *Back in 1923, with the Ottawa Senators holding the Stanley Cup and all four clubs having prospered,*

> *rumours circulated which shook the then six year-old NHL to its foundations. They were to the effect that the Hamilton and Toronto clubs would bolt from the NHL and enter an International League with Cleveland, Buffalo, Pittsburg and several other United States cities. Les Canadiens and Ottawa Senators, according to unconfirmed reports, were to be left out in the cold. However, the Ottawa and Montreal clubs came back with the bluff that they would take in Quebec and another Montreal club, thus eliminating Toronto and Hamilton.*
>
> *There were several stormy sessions during which the fate of the NHL hung suspended in the balance, but eventually the Hamilton and Toronto clubs decided to remain with the NHL. Accordingly, at an exciting session in Montreal representatives of the four clubs agreed to carry on for five additional years and all signed to this effect. Subsequently Boston, New York, Montreal Maroons, Chicago, Detroit, Pittsburgh and Philadelphia joined, and although several clubs subsequently withdrew, the future of the National Hockey league was made secure by reason of the briefly worded scrap of paper.*

That brief Memorandum of Agreement, dated November 10, 1923 was signed by Charlie Querrie for St. Patricks, Percy Thompson for the Hamilton Professional Hockey Club, T.P. Gorman for the Ottawa Hockey Association Limited and Leo Dandurand for the Canadien Hockey Club Inc. It was witnessed by Frank Calder, President of the National Hockey League. In it, the aforementioned parties "agree herewith for a period of five years from this date to conduct a competition known as the National Hockey League for the purpose of determining and deciding the champion professional hockey club."

Tommy Gorman was one of five men who put together the original National Hockey league in 1917. He then managed the Ottawa Senators to three Stanley Cups, in the early 1920s, and he was one of four men who sat down in 1923 and secured the future of the league with that five-year agreement.

It was a pretty impressive beginning for the sports editor-turned-hockey promoter, all because of a 'phone call from George Kennedy and some timely intervention from Major John Bassett.

THE FRANK AHEARN ERA IN OTTAWA

Tommy's last season in Ottawa was in 1924, following which he headed to New York and the New York Americans. He had nothing but praise, however, for his successor in the nation's capital, one Frank Ahearn.

> *No man has ever contributed more to hockey than Mr. Frank Ahearn, long-time President of the Senators and former Member of Parliament. Frank broke into hockey in 1922 and then launched his idea of the Ottawa Auditorium. His father, the Hon. Thomas Ahearn, assisted greatly in financing the Auditorium, which was built at a cost of $485,000, most of which was underwritten by Thomas Ahearn.*
>
> *Frank purchased the Ottawa Hockey Association franchise in the National Hockey League in 1925 and carried on hockey in Ottawa, despite many setbacks, until 1935 when, after operating in St. Louis for one season he surrendered his franchise and players.*

Frank put across some exceptionally clever player transactions when at the head of the Senators, dealing such magnetic stars and future stars as Hooley Smith, Scotty Bowman, Sid Howe, and Frank 'King' Clancy. Ahearn continued professional hockey in Ottawa as long as it was possible to do so and it was with great regret that he finally transferred the Senators to St. Louis and then decided to dispose of his players and the franchise.

In the critical early days of the NHL Ahearn proved most generous. He always paid his players top salaries and he brought the Stanley Cup to Ottawa in 1927. Had it not been for Frank Ahearn it is doubtful if the Auditorium would ever have been built.

It was very difficult, of course for Ahearn and his colleagues to compete in the player market against New York, Chicago, Boston, Montreal, Detroit and Toronto but he kept his Senators right in Ottawa and in the thick of the championship race as long as it was possible to do so. Hec Kilrea and Frank Finnegan were two of his greatest 'finds.' Another was Alex Connell. Not until the Ottawa fans fell off in their patronage in fact did Mr. Ahearn decide to withdraw. "Too bad" commented Connie Smythe. "There goes the Cradle of Hockey in Canada." "Unfortunate but true" added President Frank Calder. "But Ottawa isn't now big enough for the National Hockey League. It would be unfair to ask Mr. Ahearn to continue there."

And so began a 58-year year hiatus before the National Hockey League, and the Ottawa Senators, returned to the NHL in 1992, with Ottawans Bruce Firestone, Randy Sexton and Cyril Leeder leading the charge. The Cradle of Hockey was reborn.

NEW YORK, NEW YORK

Tommy sold his interests in the Ottawa Hockey Association on January 24, 1925. He recalls:

> *They had tried to get my signature to an agreement that I would not go into hockey again for 10 years. No dice. Two days later I signed with 'Tex' Rickard to manage the New York Americans. Little did I know what I was getting into.*

The Americans had arrived in New York by a strange route. They were, in fact, the old Hamilton Tigers, whose players had gone on strike that year. The NHL had cancelled the Hamilton franchise and – lock, stock and barrel – the players went to New York to form a new team, the New York Americans.

When Tommy arrived in the big city, there was no team. Putting one together was an enormous challenge.

> *Without doubt, the organization of the New York Americans for their debut in the National Hockey League provided one of hockey's greatest adventures.*

With 'Tex' Rickard as Honorary President and Tom Duggan managing director, we had bought Joe Simpson and 'Crutchy' Morrison from Edmonton for $10,000. In those days that was big dough.

Other clubs had promised help, but it wasn't forthcoming. The season was fast approaching and the Americans had been given until October 15th to assemble a team. In desperation I finally recommended the purchase of the entire Hamilton club.

The Tigers had been suspended at the close of the 1924 season for refusing to take part in the play-offs and their future seemed uncertain. Tom Duggan and I visited Hamilton as last resort after all correspondence efforts had failed and we bought the Tigers for $75,000. At that they were a bargain for in the deal the Americans landed Jackie Forbes, Ken Randall, Charlie Langlois, Shorty Green, Red Green, Billy Burch, Eddie Bouchard, Alex McKinnan and Mickey Roach. In modern, frenzied financing Billy Burch alone would have brought $75,000.

True, the Americans didn't quite measure up to expectations in New York and missed the playoffs in their first year, but this was chiefly due to the lack of hockey facilities there. They weren't important enough for Madison Square Garden and had to train in Brooklyn, Princeton and elsewhere on the road. But the erstwhile 'Tigers' put hockey over in New York and rolled up nearly $500,000 in gate receipts for their opening campaign at the new Madison Square Garden.

> *At $75,000, plus $10,000 for Bullet Joe and Crutchy Morrison they were well worth the money.*

They firmly established hockey in New York. But, recalls Tommy,

> *We still had to sell hockey in New York. Many had never heard of the game. One of Rickard's stunts was to paper the house with free tickets to all of the lovely chorus girls of The Great White Way. He figured the men would follow and they did. But some of the girls I'll never forget, like the young lady who said "Hockey? Oh sure, I know the game. They play it on horseback, don't they?"*

Now they had a team, but how did New York get a franchise in the first place? T.P. continues:

> *The true story of how the Americans - the Amazing Amerks – entered the National Hockey League back in 1925 constitutes one of the most amazing chapters in the history of the great winter game. The man who really secured the American franchise in the NHL was Thomas J. Duggan of Montreal. Duggan applied to the NHL several times and finally produced a certified cheque for $10,000, for which he was given franchises in Boston and New York. He then sold the Boston franchise to Charles Adams for a reported $10,000.*
>
> *Duggan made several trips to New York in an effort to interest promoters in that city. He was not successful, though Tex Rickard and Col. John Hammond promised Tom that the new Madison Square Garden might be interested if Duggan would install the ice plant which, he figured, would cost approximately $80,000. Duggan and*

his American franchise were homeless, but he refused to give up and continued his desperate search.

One night he was travelling to New York on the late train when he sauntered into the smoking car. There he met a stranger named Jack Rogers, an 'importer' who made frequent trips between New York and Montreal. Tom Duggan unfolded his sad story to Jack Rogers, saying "I have the New York franchise but I can't find anyone to back me. I am about to toss in the towel." "Wait, my friend," implored the ruddy-faced Rogers. "Have you ever heard of Big Bill Dwyer?" "No" replied Duggan. "Do you think he would be interested?" "I will introduce you to him tomorrow," said Rogers. "Meet us in the Claridge Hotel at one o'clock. I think Bill would like to get into hockey with you. I have seen some games in Montreal and the sport is fascinating."

Next day, at the appointed time, Tom Duggan and Bill Dwyer shook hands in the old Claridge Hotel. And that was how Tom Duggan solved his financial problem and how Bill Dwyer secured a partnership in the New York Americans. Within two weeks they had signed a deal with Madison Square Garden and Duggan notified the NHL that the Americans would be ready to operate in the fall of 1925. He signed me as manager.

The franchise was in place. A home had been found. A team had been put together. But was New York ready?

On December 15, 1925, before the most glamourous audience that had ever witnessed a hockey game, Tom

> *Duggan and Bill Dwyer presented the Americans and Les Canadiens at Madison Square Garden. Colourful bands of the West Point cadets and the Governor-General's Foot Guards, bearing their respective flags, marched to center ice and played their national anthems, while the jam-packed Garden went wild with enthusiasm.*

And with the ensuing face-off between the Amerks' Billy Burch and the amazing Howie Morenz of Les Canadiens, hockey had arrived in New York.

T.P. AND HIS NEW YORK BOSSES

For a man from little old Ottawa (population about 125,000) life in New York (population about six million) must have been a wondrous adventure. His career there brought him into close contact with men like 'Tex' Rickard, the legendary 'Tex' Rickard, maybe the greatest boxing promoter of all time and the architect of the Madison Square Garden which was built in 1925. Then there was Big Bill Dwyer, a sensational character in his own right. And Tom Duggan, the man who got hockey started in New York.

> *Tex Rickard appeared skeptical about the success of hockey in New York, but that magnificent turn-out on Opening Night convinced him otherwise. Then along came the Rangers, bitter rivalry and financial strife. Tex was always the peacemaker. Soon however the handwriting was on the wall. They wanted to eliminate the Americans.*
>
> *In the fall of 1928 Bill Dwyer's Americans had risen to great popularity. Money was really rolling in. We had a*

little suite in the Forrest Hotel on Jacob's Beach and Tex would drop in regularly on his way home. New York was supposedly dry in those days but we always managed to have a cocktail for Tex. One evening he stepped in, holding his side. "Sharp pains here" he commented, accepting the glass. "I'm travelling to Florida to open our dog track. Going to have my appendix out on my return next week." We shook hands warmly and he remarked "Keep those Americans out front. I will see you on my return."

Tex went to Florida, was stricken there and died on the operating table. Some young surgeon had bungled it. They brought him home to Madison Square Garden, which was banked gallery-high in flowers, while sorrowing pugilists, bicycle riders, wrestlers, sports writers and politicians wept openly.

"To my friend Tom.." signed by the legendary Tex Rickard.

If Tex Rickard had a spectacular Madison Square Garden send-off, Tom Duggan's ending was the polar opposite. T.P. reminisces:

> *It was in the Windsor Hotel in Montreal that I last saw Tom Duggan. He appeared greatly depressed and informed me that he had just been deprived of all his stock in the Mount Royal Race Track. What he told me was unbelievable. "Those racketeers have cleaned me out" he said. "Yesterday at the King's Park Club House they forced me to sign everything over to them."*
>
> *"Why did you do it Tom?" I asked in amazement. "Why didn't you take your lawyer to the conference?" "He couldn't have done any good" concluded Duggan. "They had a gun in my stomach!" The next month I stepped off a train in Syracuse to meet my family. "Tom Duggan died last night" was the first thing they told me. "It was a sudden heart attack."*
>
> *Poor Tom Duggan. Formerly a millionaire, he died practically broke. No one from New York showed up to sympathize with the grand little family that big-hearted Duggan had left to mourn him. Two years later, thanks to the RCMP and FBI, I learned more about the Mount Royal situation. People operating the Black River course in Montreal were representing the 'Lucky Luciano' syndicate.*

Luciano, of course was one of America's most notorious gangsters. No wonder Tom Duggan did not take a lawyer to that meeting.

Big Bill Dwyer was a boss of a different sort. He was an early Prohibition gangster and bootlegger in New York in the 1920s and was sometimes referred to as the King of the Rum Runners. From his fabulous profits he used some of the cash to buy sports properties, including the New York Americans. But he had his run-ins with the law, and Tommy recalls one:

> *Attorney Joseph Shalleck acted as Bill Dwyer's attorney for some time and also as solicitor for the New York Americans hockey club. Shalleck put up a desperate legal battle when Big Bill slipped into difficulties with prohibition enforcement officers, but he finally lost out to 'Mr. Whiskers' as he used to call Uncle Sam, and Bill was forced to complete a two year visit to a jail in Atlanta. Bill was missing from Broadway and fans in the upper bleachers at Madison Square Garden were continually shouting down to the Americans' bench: "Hey Gorman, did you get your orders from Atlanta tonight?"*
>
> *Came that bright afternoon in the summer of 1928 when Bill Dwyer stepped out of Atlanta a free man, though there were still a couple of income tax affairs to be straightened out. Joe Shalleck, I remember, called me from his office at Broadway and 42nd Street. "Bill is coming home and he wants you to take complete charge of his Americans again. Fly down and we will drive out to see him." Shalleck had a Cadillac convertible. The sun shone brightly on this particular day and we motored out to Belle Harbor. Shalleck unfolded some of Dwyer's plans for the rebuilding of the Americans. "It means a lot to him and will re-establish him in New York" he emphasized.*

Within a quarter mile of Bill Dwyer's lovely residence in Belle Harbor we spotted dozens of parked cars. It was impossible to get near his home. Hundreds had turned out to greet the prodigal son. Bill's green lawn was jammed, the sidewalks were teeming with people. It looked in fact, something like a wedding or funeral. And there on the verandah sat the inimitable Bill Dwyer. Mrs. Dwyer, a dazzling blonde, stood on one side and he had a big collie dog on the other. Bill kept shaking hands with his friends with his right and patting the dog with his left. Bill's reception continued all afternoon and that night he took us out to a gorgeous beach restaurant for a shore dinner – probably his first in many moons!

Within a few weeks we had reconstructed the Americans. The rejuvenated Americans immediately clicked and they held first place for the greater part of the season and slipped back to second when Les Canadiens, led by Howie Morenz, closed with a terrific rush. Lionel Conacher was a leader of the Americans. It proved my last season with the star-spangled puck chasers. That season of 1928-29 proved the best season they ever enjoyed.

It had been a tumultuous but exciting four years on Broadway, and Tommy remembers some of the events which shaped his time there.

You didn't have to be very observant to realize that Bill Dwyer had other interests besides hockey. He had a million-dollar home, and a group of very competent-looking men accompanied him everywhere. We were training the Americans in 1928 in New Haven and there

> *was a 'phone call from New York. It was Marty Shenker, one of the American directors. "We want you to arrange an exhibition match for next Sunday night" said Marty. "Bill and all the mob will be there. Make sure you have the match. This is vitally important."*

So T.P., as he had been instructed, arranged a game with Springfield.

> *The New York party arrived about five o'clock the night of the game and Bill threw a sumptuous party with the sky the limit. They brought with them hockey writers, photographers and radio men. After an elaborate dinner they adjourned to the arena and occupied seats in the front row. At the start of the game Big Bill himself faced off the puck for photographers while his companions worked their way conspicuously into the pictures as the flashbulbs flashed and the crowd cheered.*

Tommy's team won the game and Bill Dwyer and his companions headed back to New York in their Cadillacs. As T.P. recalls,

> *At the time, I wondered why so much money and effort should have gone into publicizing an unimportant exhibition game. Next morning, a Monday, the New York tabloids published photos of Big Bill and his pals at the New Haven game. This, of course was all in the sports sections. On their front pages, in screaming type, these same papers headlined 'ARNOLD ROTHSTEIN MURDERED LAST NIGHT IN PARK CENTRAL HOTEL.'*

Rothstein, a notorious New York racketeer, businessman and gambler, was the kingpin of the Jewish mob in New York and widely considered to be the founding father of organized crime in the United States. He died on November 6, 1928, after being shot, apparently over a huge poker debt. His murderer was never found. Big Bill and his pals, of course, were at a hockey game in New Haven.

> *Everything happened to the Americans. We were in a train wreck in Altoona, en route from Pittsburgh and on one occasion when we were to have played in Fort Erie the arena there collapsed. There were no practice hours available at Madison Square Garden. One morning two of my players came pounding on my door. They were in overcoats, pyjamas, slippers and caps. "There was an explosion in our apartment," they explained. "We lost everything." One of our players deserted the team because he became homesick; another because his wife felt there would be too much temptation for him in the Big City; a swarthy-looking citizen rushed into our dressing room, shouting for one of our defencemen. It was difficult to know what he really wanted, but not difficult to see the big, gleaming knife he had hitched to his belt. We immediately transferred said defenceman to one of the far west clubs.*

Tom Gorman thought that the New York fans were among the best in the world, but when the Americans took to the ice in 1925 there were more than a few skeptics in the crowd.

> *Quite a lot of money sometimes changed hands and some of the fans had foolish suspicions that all was not on the up and up, so to speak. Often, in fact when goalkeeper Jakie Forbes missed a long shot or even when he failed to block an impossible drive, down from the top gallery*

would come the cry "It's in the bag, it's in the bag!" Madison Square Garden soon became known around the league as The Goalkeeper's Graveyard. Even great blockers like John Ross Roach, Lorne Chabot and Roy Worters heard the derisive shouts and several cracked under the strain.

Fireman Alex Connell, on the other hand, loved to perform in New York. In one season he registered three shutouts there. Chuck Gardiner, Bill Durnan, Frankie Brimsek, Tiny Thompson and Turk Broda all starred beneath the bright lights at the famous Garden.

And there were all kinds of non-stop promotions to keep New Yorkers interested. Ambulances would line up outside Madison Square Garden to take away the injured players; Bullet Joe Simpson related to the New York media how he once played in Edmonton at sixty below zero. He then told them how he had travelled sixty miles on snowshoes to make a train connection to New York. The story was told how Crutchy Morrison had shot three bears in his back yard in Manitoba just before leaving for New York. But evil days fell on the 'Amazing Americans.'

At one point Bill had refused an offer of $350,000 for the team, but came the day at an NHL meeting in Detroit when he had to admit he was head over heels in debt and could not keep up his payments on the star-spangled team. They took away his franchise and began dividing up his players. It was a cruel day for Bill, the man who had put up $80,000 for the ice plant at Madison Square Garden and who had originally brought big-time hockey to New York. "We haven't even got car fare back" said

> *Bill, standing alone in the lobby of the Brooke-Cadillac Hotel while the governors of the NHL wrote him off in the boardroom of the hotel. They were not entirely without generosity. They advanced him $200 towards his expenses. What a melancholy exit!*

The New York Rangers had arrived in town, and Tommy's reputation as a sports promoter had reached as far as the west coast. Horse racing interests in southern California made him an offer he couldn't refuse.

THE ALLURE OF MEXICO

For millions of people the Great Depression, which began with the stock market crash of October, 1929, and lasted for a decade, was the worst of times. Not so for Tommy Gorman, however. That era was one of the most exciting times in his adventurous life. He had already made a name for himself in the east as a hockey executive, promoter extraordinaire and a knowledgeable racing man. By 1928 his fame had spread to the west coast of the United States and on Christmas Day of that year he was hired as assistant manager at the continent's newest and most spectacular thoroughbred race track, in Tijuana, Mexico, just across the border from San Diego, California. It was called Agua Caliente.

That racing palace was financed and built by wealthy Americans including Sunny Jim Coffroth, a member of the Tijuana gambling establishment, Baron Long, a Los Angeles nightclub owner, and Wirt Bowman, owner of a Tijuana gambling business.

Agua Caliente.

Caliente thrived. It opened in 1929 (just before the market crash) with Gorman playing a prominent role. It attracted all of the big Hollywood movie stars of the day – Charlie Chaplin, Rita Hayworth, Laurel and Hardy, and a host of others – and it attracted international attention when the track put up a purse of $100,000 added – unheard-of –for the Agua Caliente Handicap. It was at the time the biggest purse in thoroughbred racing, anywhere in the world. For four years, Gorman and Caliente did wonderfully well in the sunny, warm northern Mexico climate. But much of the success was due to the fact that drinking, gambling and horse-racing were illegal in many states, California included – and that was about to change.

California legalized all of the above, and construction of the magnificent Santa Anita race track near Los Angeles was to be completed in time for the 1934 racing season. The writing was on the wall for Agua Caliente. No longer would the hordes of Americans who loved the action at the race track be forced to trek into Mexico. The movie stars, their entourages and thousands of ordinary racing fans would be able to enjoy their beloved sport much closer to home.

Jim Coleman, one of Canada's most respected sports writers, wrote a marvelous book entitled *Long Ride on a Hobby Horse: Memoirs of a Sporting Life*[18] and he devoted considerable space to Tommy's comings and goings. About the impending decline of Agua Caliente and Gorman's sixth sense, Coleman wrote: "Coincidentally, the 1932 renewal of the Agua Caliente Handicap had been won by Phar Lap, probably the best horse ever bred in the Antipodes. Phar Lap was a giant of a thoroughbred and outclassed the U.S. steeds which ran against him at Agua Caliente. Gorman, sensing that the best days of Agua Caliente were numbered, hit upon a brilliant scheme. He signed a contract with Phar Lap's owner to take the Australian wonder horse on an exhibition tour of the major tracks in North America. It was a 'can't miss' plan because Phar Lap had generated tremendous curiosity among sports enthusiasts; with the exception of news-reel clips in motion picture houses, more than 200,000,000 Americans had never seen the Champion From Down Under in action."

Phar Lap, the giant Australian wonder horse at Agua Caliente.

18 Toronto, Key Porter Books, 1990.

Coleman continues: "Gorman and the horse's owners were expecting to split a juicy melon. They had guarantees of more than $200,000 from eastern tracks. Then something disastrous occurred--Phar Lap died! Just before the tour was to begin, the horse was grazing on some grass outside his barn at Menlo Park, California. The barn had been spray-painted the previous day and some of the paint—which contained arsenate of lead—had blown onto the grass. Phar Lap died of lead poisoning."

The cause of Phar Lap's death has never been proven conclusively. Coleman's theory might be correct, but recent, more scientific theories using DNA testing point to arsenic poisoning and there are many who believed that powerful U.S mafia-led mobsters had the horse done in so he would not upset their lucrative gambling businesses. That turn of events would have destroyed a lesser man, but Gorman moved on from that disaster to some of his most spectacular hockey successes.

Gorman reflects on his dealings with the magnificent Phar Lap and the horse's entourage:

> *The tragic story of the magnificent Phar Lap has been reprinted so frequently that most Canadians and Americans are familiar with the triumphs and death of that great Australian wonder horse.*
>
> *How we heard of Phar Lap's phenomenal record on the Australian turf; how we wired owner Davis in January, 1932, and then brought the speedy gelding to Caliente; how we met him with a brass band at the Mexican border and how he cracked a track record in outrunning the finest thoroughbreds that America could produce—these facts are all recorded in many important turf books.*

However, there were other incidents concerning Phar Lap. When he first landed in Tijuana owner Davis, always nervous and impatient, rushed up saying "Gorman, we must have a pony for Phar Lap. He always likes company in his stable." Well, getting a pony at that time in Mexico wasn't so easy. Laurie Gomez and Juan Romero, after others had searched unsuccessfully, arrived back from the Sonora hills with a smile. They had found a pony and bought him for 10 pesos. My heavens! What a pony! He was the skinniest-looking four-legged creature I had ever seen; his little bones stuck out on both sides and it was evident he had not felt the impact of water for many moons. "Clean him up and take him over to Mr. Davis" I ordered the Mexican roustabouts, who seemed quite proud of their ragged capture. "He may do for the time being."

Well, that wandering bag of bones was so hungry he actually started to eat his bedding when they put him in with Phar Lap. He munched on a bucket of oats, drank all the water he could get and finally collapsed, probably excited and fatigued after his unexpected run from the mountains. And Phar Lap? He just kept looking sympathetically at his wobbling, worthless new stable mate, then stepped gently over and made friends with him.

They used to take Phar Lap for long walks early in the morning and of course Pedro the pony went along. They presented a striking contrast, this gorgeous big Australian wonder horse following his unfortunate companion who, however, had picked up considerably since his introduction to Phar Lap. They would walk for miles down the desert, usually before sunrise. Hundreds turned out to see them. "My God" said Baron Long one Sunday morning. "That's a disgraceful looking cavalcade. Get rid of that hobo immediately and I will ship you down a fine-looking pinto from our ranch in San Diego." Baron Long sent the buckskin beauty and after giving him another hearty meal, the Mexicans chased Pedro out into the wilderness.

Huge crowds followed Phar Lap. That's T.P. on the horse's back at Agua Caliente.

And what happened next in the eventful career of the great Phar Lap? Well, he kicked and he bit the new pinto pony, he refused to eat his oats and he made one dangerous lunge at owner Davis. He would, in fact, have nothing to do with his ritzy new companion from the ranch of wealthy Baron Long. And so, to pacify Phar Lap, Gomez and Romero had to ride back into the mountains again to recover that old glue factory candidate to which Phar Lap had taken a strange liking. Horse sense. Phar Lap had plenty of it.

They didn't think Phar Lap had a chance, but he carried off the Agua Caliente Handicap with ease and established himself as the greatest thoroughbred of his time. Two weeks later, with a contract from owner Davis in my briefcase I travelled east on The Chief,[19] *authorized to book Phar Lap for 'personal appearances' at Windsor, Toronto, Hamilton, Ottawa, Montreal, Chicago, New York and Saratoga. We were going to run the big Australian gelding against time, but we were going to make sure he would not be beaten.*

At Kansas City, I slipped out to buy some papers. And there in grim black type across the top of the Kansas City Star I read the startling headline 'Phar Lap, Wonder Horse, Dies at San Francisco.' I slipped back into that lower berth on The Chief and nearly died too. Davis and I would have cleaned up a million.

Perhaps the outstanding feature of the Agua Caliente Handicap on that historical day was the remarkable radio broadcast, all the way across the broad Pacific, while millions listened in. George Shilling handled the microphone and I can recall how he dramatized

19 'The Chief' ('El Capitain') was the name of the Atchison, Topeka & Santa Fe Railroad train, running daily between Los Angeles and Chicago.

the start, the early stages of the mile and a furlong contest, and then, fairly shrieking as the thundering thoroughbreds turned for the home stretch. "My God, Australia, here comes Phar Lap!"

So, they stuffed Phar Lap and prepared to ship him back to the Australian Hall of Fame. Someone at Belmont Park in New York wished me to see the lifeless giant, whom thousands crowded around. I didn't have the heart to do so. I like to remember Phar Lap, pounding down that Agua Caliente track and winning easily under Willie Elliott, who did not even have to apply his whip. It was a glorious day for Australia.

FUN AND GAMES DOWN MEXICO WAY

For Tay Pay, life in Mexico in the early part of the Dirty Thirties was interesting, to say the least. As assistant GM of the continent's greatest race track, Agua Caliente, he came into contact with the rich, the famous, the not-so-rich and the not-so-famous. He had fun with them all. And he was a close-up witness to some of the incredible antics that made the race track so much fun for him. In his memoirs, he tells this story, no doubt with a big smile as he writes:

> *We had a box in the center of the Clubhouse Terrace at Caliente. Celebrities used to gather around it and my daughter had a great time collecting autographs. If she heard of any movie star coming down she would immediately rush for that little red book. Will Rogers, Charlie Chaplin, Ronald Coleman, Barbara Stanwyck, Jean Harlow...she had 'em all. One afternoon I heard Betty calling as I passed below the Terrace. "Come on up here" she shouted. "I want you to meet Mr. Caesar." Her new friend was Edward G. Robinson.*

They made many successful motion pictures at Caliente. One morning after actor Ronald Coleman had pulled himself out of bed at seven o'clock, his director reported that he couldn't work that day. Poor fellow...he had a headache. Ronald Coleman didn't show up for the next three days. He had gone fishing!

In that movie they used a horse in one of the race track scenes and it crashed into the camera truck. "Terrible, terrible" cried C.B. Irwin, its owner. "I would not have sold that gelding for $10,000. Send for my lawyer!" The Hollywood movie company immediately settled for the Ten Grand. That dead horse had been running in $500 claiming races. He wasn't worth $300. How C.B. smiled when he looked at that $10,000 cheque. "Let's go and eat" said the 300 pound owner from Cheyenne, Wyoming. "There's one born every minute."

Tommy tells this story too, about the Agua Caliente president, James Crofton:

We were anxiously awaiting, one sunny afternoon, James Crofton's return from Mexico City where he had gone on important business. I answered the telephone. "Got into a little poker game on the way west" said Jim. "They cleaned me. Bring me down $10,000. I'm going on to San Francisco with these gentlemen." Next night he called from the City of the Golden Gate. "Got it all back and more with it" said Crofton. "Meet me at the airport with that I.O.U." On another occasion Crofton handed me a package at the Jamaica race track in New York. "Give that to my secretary in Tijuana" he said,

> *"and don't lose it." Good thing I didn't misplace that little brown parcel. It contained $60,000. Jim had evidently picked some winners.*

So, in the midst of the Great Depression there was, in some circles at least, a lot of cash flying around. And wherever there's cash, there's bound to be some interested observers, not all of them choirboys. Al Capone visited Caliente on Gorman's watch. He did not stick around for long, though, and caused no trouble. Another visitor was Jack ('Legs') Diamond, an Irish-American gangster who survived a number of attempts on his life, causing him to be known as the Clay Pigeon of the Underworld. These two were among the most notorious criminals in U.S. history.

Gorman had a reputation as a pretty good judge of talent, and of character, but he did not always get it right. One character in particular stood out.

> *The stranger in the smart blue jacket seemed to have dropped out of the sky, just as we were trying desperately to get things in shape for the opening of the summer race meet at Caliente. All he wanted was a job. We didn't even discuss salary. Never was I happier to have someone to help with the ticket distributions, badge writing, program production and staff re-organization. Gosh, but was he efficient. Nothing appeared to ruffle him. Every night his cash balanced to the penny. He handled a heap of money too. He told me he lived in Tijuana with his wife and baby. He could drive a car, type, and he knew shorthand. There wasn't anything, in fact, he didn't seem to qualify for. His wife looked pretty as a southern lullaby and his little boy was bright and clean.*

Then came the inevitable crash. Someone had recognized him. "Where did you get that man Hobson you have up at the track?" Wirt Bowman demanded after I had obeyed an SOS signal from his office. "Does he handle money?" inquired Mr. Bowman cautiously while Jim Crofton stepped in with a circular photo of my able assistant in his right hand. "Hundreds each day," I admitted "and he has never been short one peso." "Thought you might like to know" continued Mr. Bowman, "every police officer in Arizona is looking for him. He robbed a bank over there of $100,000. Kidnap him over to the United States side and you can earn a $20,000 reward."

I guess I paled somewhat at the shock because I liked the man and he certainly had rescued me. "What shall I do?" I asked. "What do you want to do? You are the boss" replied Mr. Bowman, an immensely wealthy American who had married a beautiful Mexican girl many years ago. Before I could reply big-hearted Jim Crofton stepped up. He never failed to come to my rescue in a crisis. He tore up the photograph. "Keep the fellow on the job" declared Crofton "but tell him not to cross the international boundary. They can't touch him on this side. To blazes with their reward!"

Last time I saw him my guy with the blue jacket was handling the Agua Caliente payroll. I don't know whatever became of that $100,000. He was still shopping on the Mexican side, and every Christmas I received a pretty card postmarked Tijuana.

Maybe Tommy got this one right, too. Hollywood superstars and Mexican roustabouts. Big-time gangsters and big-time gambling bosses. A phenomenal race horse. A bank robber as his assistant. This part of T.P.'s career only lasted about four years, but what a four years it was!

THE WINDY CITY

Tommy's stay in Chicago with the Black Hawks was short—everyone's stay with the Hawks was short in those days—but it was hugely successful, culminating in a Stanley Cup win in 1933-34.

The Hawks joined the league in 1926 with a motley collection of players, and most hockey fans thought they were something of a joke. The president of the hockey club, Major Frederic B. McLaughlin, hired and fired his coaches on a whim and in their first 12 years of existence the Hawks had 13 different coaches. The mercurial McLaughlin's wife added to the problems faced by Hawk coaches. She had been a member of one of the most famous ballroom-dance teams in the United States, but she apparently had become an instant expert on all things hockey. She sat behind the bench at all home games and made her opinions loudly known to the poor, suffering men employed by the Major to coach his hockey team.

When T.P. took over behind the Hawks bench on January 14, 1933, he was the team's third coach that season, a season consisting of just 48 games. How did he get to that precarious position? With not a little self-promotion, it seems. He could foresee the decline of Agua Caliente.

His dreams of making a fortune with Phar Lap died with the horse. He would need a job. So he fired off a bunch of letters, purportedly written by sports writers from across America, extolling the virtues of one Thomas Patrick Gorman as the man who could turn around the sad-sack franchise. After just one meeting in Chicago, McLaughlin hired him.

The financial state of the Black Hawks was uncertain. T.P. recalls:

> *The Major had experienced troubles in financing his Chicago Black Hawks. Out at Arlington Park race track one sunny afternoon he accidentally bumped into Joe Cattarinich, then owner of the Canadien hockey club, whom he had met at several NHL meetings. He unloaded his troubles. "Some of the Chicago gangsters are trying to secure control of the Black Hawks" he explained. "They already own the Stadium."*
>
> *"How much do you need?" asked the suave Mr. Cattaranich. "Fifty thousand dollars" replied the Black Hawk president. "Just stay there until after this next race" requested Cattaranich. "I'll see what I can do." Ten minutes later Joe returned and handed McLaughlin $50,000 in crisp American bills. He didn't even ask for an IOU!*
>
> *When I signed to manage Chicago, Major McLaughlin said "I owe Joe Cattaranich $50,000 and I'm going to pay back every cent as soon as possible." He did this within two years as the Black Hawks entered the Stanley Cup in 1934 and crowds began to flock back into the new Stadium to see them play. In the summer of 1936, Joe Cattaranich handed me a cheque for $10,000 in payment of a race track account. It was the last of the Black Hawk*

> *settlements of that $50,000 loan. "McLaughlin will smile when he sees your name on the back of that cheque" commented Mr. Cattaranich. Thus, with a handshake and a $50,000 cash loan, the Black Hawks were able to continue.*

Tommy knew right away who he needed to make the Black Hawks into a respectable hockey team. He needed Lionel Conacher, the very talented defenceman then playing for the Montreal Maroons. He immediately traded for Conacher and only 15 months later, the sad-sack laughing stock from the Windy City, the Chicago Black Hawks, became Stanley Cup champions. Behind the magnificent goaltending of Chuck Gardiner the Hawks defeated Les Canadiens, the Maroons and Detroit en route to their improbable Cup. Gorman, Conacher, Gardiner and the rest of the team became civic heroes. Perhaps the only person in Chicago who was not over the moon with excitement was Major McLaughlin. T.P., it seems, was making executive decisions with respect to the hockey team without bothering to consult with the Major.

T.P. is in the middle, back row.

So, having put together the team which brought Chicago its first-ever Stanley Cup, Gorman was fired! No matter, because the agile Tay Pay was on his way to Montreal the very next season to coach and manage the Montreal Maroons. He took Conacher and Cy Wentworth with him, and together they did the impossible. They won the Stanley Cup again, for the second consecutive year, with different teams in different cities. Gorman's portion of that feat, the coaching part, is still unequalled in the NHL, some 80 years later. He recalls his first visit back to Chicago after winning the Cup:

> *Even though we had jumped to Montreal Maroons in the fall of 1934, Lionel Conacher and I thought we would still be heroes in Chicago. Hadn't we won the Stanley Cup for the Windy City and the Black Hawks? Hadn't we helped make Chicago the hottest hockey city in the NHL? Why shouldn't they like us? And so we were pleased to learn that, on the occasion of the first visit of the battling Maroons to Chicago, Black Hawk fans in the upper bleachers planned to honour us. We anxiously awaited the initial appearance of the rebuilt Maroons in the big Stadium.*
>
> *"What do you think they will give us?" Cy Wentworth inquired. Wentworth had gone from Chicago to the Maroons with Gorman and Conacher. "Probably watches" replied The Big Train, then in his glory as an all-star defenceman in the NHL. And after the marauding Maroons had skated around a few times, down from the top gallery came a big shining object, a glittering piece of steel, attached to which was a cardboard square bearing this inscription: 'To*

Gorman, Conacher and Wentworth, this is the key to Lake Michigan. Go and jump in!' What a tribute! But we had our revenge. After the Maroons beat the Black Hawks in the championship play-offs, Conacher skated around the Stadium, making motions with his hands and shouting: "Turn out the lights, Chicago. You won't need them any more this season!"

Tommy's stay in Chicago was short, but not without its adventures.

Major McLaughlin didn't like me staying at a certain hotel in Chicago. I stayed there because a former Ottawa man was assistant manager and everyone there appeared kind to me. "It's full of gamblers and gangsters" McLaughlin warned me. "One of these fine nights they'll take you for a ride." They didn't. I never had an unpleasant word with any of the Sherman Hotel patrons. I told them honestly if I thought the Black Hawks could win or lose. They were gentlemanly and grateful. Usually after a game we mingled with the lobby-sitters, enjoying coffee and sandwiches at the little bar. It seemed pleasant and soothing, particularly after the mad roars in the Stadium. I couldn't remember all their names but no one ever offered any offence and they began patronizing the Black Hawk games. I could spot them from the Chicago bench.

Then there came that night when the Black Hawks defeated Detroit. One of my hotel acquaintances, who I had only known as 'Mac,' came along and slapped me on the back. He had a gorgeous little package of femininity with him, smothered in mink and diamonds. I noticed

> *how several Chicago detectives crowded around. "What am I going to do with you?" Major McLaughlin subsequently asked. "That guy you were chumming with tonight was Machine Gun Jack McGurn."*

Tommy clearly did not realize it, but his new pal Jack was a Sicilian-American mobster and a key member of Al Capone's Chicago outfit. Machine Gun Jack was assassinated in Chicago in 1936. It brought to mind his recollection of Tom Duggan's attempt to bring dog racing to the Windy City.

> *Duggan and his crew were enjoying a room-service meal at the Morrison when his secretary answered a knock on the door. Two rugged-looking men stood there, and one handed in a note. It read: 'If you like the birds and the flowers, get out of Chicago within twenty-four hours.' No signature was on it, but none was necessary. Tom and his crew departed that night. They weren't going to argue with Al Capone over a few dogs.*
>
> *But Chicago wasn't so bad. Everyone proved friendly and I left them the Stanley Cup.*

That was Gorman's fourth Cup win. Next, on to Montreal.

THE BIG TRAIN

Lionel Conacher, aka "The Big Train", was named Canada's top male athlete of the first half of the twentieth century, and with good reason. His spectacular exploits on the ice and on the playing fields earned him entry into The Canadian Sports Hall of Fame, the Canadian Football Hall of Fame, the Canadian Lacrosse Hall of Fame and the Hockey Hall of Fame. He was one tremendous package of brilliant athletic diversity.

Such recognition nearly failed to occur, however. Conacher played hockey for T.P. in New York, but trouble arose in the Big Apple for the highly-skilled athlete. Gorman remembers his lengthy relationship with Conacher this way:

> *Lionel became manager of the Amazing Americans in the summer of 1929 after I had forsaken the bright lights of Broadway for the hot sands of Mexico. Unfortunately, things became very dismal in the camp of the star-spangled boys.*
>
> *Then came the spring of 1930. Back in the east again, I ventured into the Americans' suite on Jacob's Beach.*

Naturally, a post-mortem on the Vanishing Americans soon came about. "You had better see Lionel Conacher" one of the American directors suggested. "He is in pretty bad shape. Painful cut on his right leg. They say he may never walk again." 'Connie' was really in terrible shape. He had been painfully gashed in the last game the Americans had played, the wound had festered and The Big Train seemed in hopeless order. Someone had actually warned him that a tendon had been cut and that he might be permanently lame. And unfortunately, working for that notorious New York boot-legger Bill Dwyer had led to a serious drinking problem for Conacher. "How about going back to Montreal, Connie?" I suggested. "You really need a change of scenery and some of the best surgical attention."

Connie was stubborn at first, but finally consented and I arranged for a drawing room on the night train to Montreal that night. I also contacted Dr. Agret McKay, then chief physician for the Maroons and told him the story. "Ship him up to me. I will do my best" commented Dr. McKay.

So the legendary Conacher arrived back in Montreal that bright Saturday morning. Dr. McKay met him as arranged and proceeded to affect [sic], in several ways, a really magical cure. Lionel Conacher had taken his last drink. From then he went on to glory. He had one rough season with the Maroons, due to injuries but he came back with a vengeance to help win the Stanley Cup for Chicago in 1934 and for the Maroons in 1935. He was also a bulwark of the Maroon team which won the championship in 1936, only to lose out to the sensational Detroit Red Wings in the Stanley Cup play-offs. What a genuine athlete he was!

And so, from a seemingly hopeless wreck at New York on a spring morning in 1930 Lionel Conacher went on to his greatest triumphs. Stanley Cups, league championships, and the Hart Trophy. They all became his because he kept his solemn promise and avoided liquor completely. His temptations were great, but Lionel met them all with a kindly smile. "No thanks," The Big Train would say. "I have had my share of that stuff. It's bad for my back-checking."

Lionel Conacher.

For T.P., making trades was part of life for a general manager. He made many, but his trade for Conacher to play in Chicago was, he said, "my greatest trade."

> *Our Black Hawks finished out of the NHL play-offs in the season of 1933, so we determined to make changes. I told Major McLaughlin I would like to land Lionel Conacher from Montreal Maroons, which was easier said than done. Conacher had been waived out of the NHL and I thought he would be valuable for Chicago. He did not appear to be in the good graces of Eddie Gerard, then the capable and popular manager of the Maroons. I learned, however that the Maroons were sweet on "Teddy" Graham, who had starred on the Chicago defence. I negotiated cautiously with Maroons and, though I will never understand what caused them to do so, they eventually agreed to exchange Conacher for Graham. "Conacher is over the hill," one of the Maroons executives argued. "We are getting a good young defenceman for an old-timer."*
>
> *Out at Blue Bonnets that afternoon I told Senator Raymond that we had traded Graham for Conacher. He was then president of the Canadian Arena Company but not an officer of the Maroons. "They must be crazy" Senator Raymond commented. "I never heard of Graham." Nevertheless the Graham for Conacher exchange materialized. Conacher had his finest season and Chicago went on to win the Stanley Cup. He also received all-star rating. Graham was used only sparingly by Maroons, who we trimmed in the*

play-offs. "That guy Gorman" wrote Elmer Ferguson in the Montreal Herald, "he traded a row-boat for a battleship."

Yes, Graham for Conacher was my most classical player exchange. Next season I took charge of the Maroons and when the season got under way, there stood Lionel Conacher in the Maroons' dressing room. "You just can't get rid of me" declared the famous Big Train, stepping out for his first match of the 1934-35 season in which he contributed immensely towards winning another Stanley Cup. He was the greatest of all Canadian athletes.

He was a bit mischievous, too.

Colonel Herbert Molson, one of the finest men I ever knew, once accompanied the Maroons to Chicago. On the return journey, the Colonel was pleased when Lionel insisted the Colonel take the only drawing room on the car. After we had gone through customs Lionel entered the compartment. "Excuse me Colonel, would you mind standing up for just a moment?" asked Conacher. Puzzled, the Colonel stood up. Lionel then began hauling out contraband material from under the Colonel's bed, a new rifle, fishing rod, reels, and even a small radio. "You scoundrel," said the Colonel. "I wouldn't have slept a wink if I'd known that was there."

After his playing days were over, Conacher went on to become an MPP in the Ontario government, and later became a Member of Parliament in Ottawa. During the 1954 Parliament Hill softball game between the parliamentary press gallery and MP's Conacher banged out a single but his competitive nature saw him try to stretch it into a triple. It was to be his last hurrah. He suffered a heart attack at third base and died soon thereafter. He was just 54.

BACK TO MONTREAL – AND THREE MORE CUPS

If, in fact, Gorman was fired from the Chicago job as some writers suggested, he didn't give any hint of it in his memoirs. He had been in near-constant contact with Senator Raymond in Montreal for several months, so he had prepared himself to take his leave from Chicago.

> *Chicago Black Hawks had just beaten Detroit Red Wings for the Stanley Cup when the management of the Montreal Maroons was offered to me. ... After the Black Hawks carried off the Stanley Cup I handed in my resignation to Major McLaughlin. He had always treated me splendidly, but I preferred to be at Montreal, which was closer to Ottawa. In any event I had succeeded in my two chief ambitions at Chicago. We had won the Stanley Cup and Joe Cattarinich had been paid back his $50,000. "You won't last one year in Montreal," Joe warned me. "That is the toughest job in North America."*

And maybe it was. The Great Depression was still in full swing, the world was rushing headlong towards World War II, Gorman didn't speak much French in a very French-speaking city, and the Maroons had not managed to wow the hockey-wise denizens of that great metropolis. In fact, the Maroons themselves failed to make it past 1938 despite winning the Cup in Tommy's first year there as coach, his fifth Cup win. The horrible economic times forced the Canadian Arena Company to make a decision: kill off the Maroons, or Les Canadiens. They elected to close up the Maroons.

That club had its share of characters, and of lighter moments despite the financial difficulties. Tommy relates a few of those stories:

> *One bright morning in the winter of 1937 the Maroons went through a strenuous two hour practice at The Forum before being allowed to skate off. Jerry Shannon and Yip Bradley however requested that they be allowed to remain on for a few more minutes. I tossed them a puck and went inside to console our exhausted Maroons, who were trying to break out of a losing streak. Remember that Bradley and Shannon were the only two players on the ice. Five minutes later they both stepped in, covered with blood. "What happened?" demanded trainer Bill O'Brien in amazement. "We collided at centre ice," explained Shannon.*
>
> *On another occasion, same dressing room, same cocky team. In they trooped, after an overtime loss. "Cheer up, fellows" remarked the irrepressible Hooley Smith. "We can't win 'em all." They had just dropped their sixth straight game. Once, a group of them went out duck-hunting in Winnipeg before daylight. "Any luck,*

> *fellows?" Jimmie Ward asked on their return. "Well" answered Cy Wentworth with a broad smile, "Smith shot the decoy, Conacher just missed our guide and Northcott nearly drowned himself."*

A playful bunch were those Maroons, but they had also gained a reputation around the NHL for their toughness.

> *I stood in the ticket line at Detroit one night. "Will it be a good game?" a sweet young lass asked her escort. "Either that or one hell of a fight," he replied. "The Maroons are in town."*

It was a well-earned reputation. Conacher himself added to the intrigue of the battling Maroons, as Tommy recalls:

> *One particular game, illiterate fans on the south side of Madison Square Garden kept up a running fire of abuse at Lionel Conacher. They finally went to extremes whereupon, with less than a minute to go, The Big Train, skates and all, hurdled the dasher, grabbed two of the most abusive of the irate spectators and managed to get in six or eight staggering wallops before Garden police dragged him back. Connie certainly silenced those critics. After the game, Cy Wentworth, who never won a fight in all his career, commented: "It's a good thing you have me on your side, Conacher. I will never let anyone hurt you!"*

Conacher and Gorman, in Montreal with the Maroons.

The colourful Maroons folded, but T.P. was not going anywhere this time around.

> *Maroons dropped out of the picture in 1938 and after Les Canadiens had floundered hopelessly for two years, during which they dropped nearly $200,000, the entire Canadien re-organization was dropped in my lap. Every player on the Canadien team except 'Toe' Blake was waived out of the NHL, after which we had to tackle a terrific re-building job. Had we not been successful, the Forum would have been transferred into a garage or warehouse, so discouraged were the directors.*

And what a rebuilding it was, so powerful that it set the stage for some of the greatest hockey teams and most exciting players the game has ever known. The cornerstone was put in place in 1940 by Gorman with a significant assist from Hector ('Toe') Blake.[20]

---

20 Blake acquired the nickname 'Toe' thanks to his younger sister who, as a child, was unable to pronounce his name correctly, choosing 'Hectoe'. It stuck.

With the coming of Dick Irvin, however, and the introduction of Elmer Lach, Bill Durnan, Jack Adams, Maurice Richard, Johnny Quilty and many others Les Canadiens played before capacity crowds and the Forum returned to prosperity.

"You and Toe Blake carried out a terrific job up there in Montreal" said Art Ross during the last NHL meeting I attended in New York. "They ought to give you the key to City Hall." I refused to accept any cut from the play-off pool and Canadien players subsequently gave me a splendid traveling case which I still treasure among my souvenirs. 'Toe,' incidentally, has never been given the credit he deserves for the success of Les Canadiens in the heart-breaking years of World War ll. They should hang up a big oil painting of 'The Old Lamplighter' in the main lobby of The Forum.

Blake went on to an incredible Hall of Fame coaching career with Les Canadiens and undoubtedly has his picture prominently displayed in the Bell Centre in Montreal.[21] It was not always apparent that Blake would succeed, though. In the beginning, the opposite seemed more likely. As T.P. remembers,

When Montreal Maroons invaded St. Louis for their first appearance there in October, 1935, we tossed over the boards, after the game had been cinched in the third period, the clumsiest, most-unlikely-to-make-good forward the National Hockey League had ever seen. He fell all over himself first time out, bumped into his own

21 The Bell Centre replaced The Forum as the home rink for Les Canadiens in 1996.

> *players, tripped and fell flat on his face several times. He had a peculiar method of skating, his stickhandling was poor and at no time did he look like a prospect.*
>
> *"Where did that bush-leaguer come from?" someone shouted from the St. Louis bench. "Did you pick him up in the wilds near Winnipeg?" But the same player improved as if by magic, on the return of the Maroons to Montreal. He was farmed out to Providence and subsequently used in a deal by which he became Canadien property, overcoming all of his handicaps to become one of the greatest left wingers in hockey, an all-star who figured on several Stanley Cup teams.*

That clumsy player was, of course, Toe Blake, one of the greatest names in the history of the sport.

Another busy day running the Montreal Forum.

As Gorman engineered the rebuilding of the Canadiens, perhaps his most important signing in the early stages was Dick Irvin, who was named coach in 1940 after spending eight years in Toronto under the watchful eye of Major Conn Smythe. Irvin had become weary of the Major's interfering ways and Gorman persuaded him to come to Montreal and give the Canadiens a try. He was instrumental in the rebuilding process, working hand-in-hand with T.P. and Toe Blake to give Montrealers a team of which they could be proud. They had set their sights on a winger named Norm Larson.

> *In the spring of 1940, after we had signed Dick Irvin to coach Les Habitants,*[22] *I negotiated with Lester Patrick, then head of the Rangers, for a winger named Norm Larson. He came to Montreal, registered at the Queen's Hotel and I hurried down to see him. I liked Larson's appearance and told him that I would correspond further with the Rangers. A tall, rangy-looking youngster was standing near the news stand. "There's a pretty good prospect too," said Larson. "His name is Elmer Lach. Toronto Maple Leafs tried him out last year, but sent him back to Saskatchewan. I'd like to see him get another chance."*
>
> *Less than an hour later Elmer Lach appeared on the Canadiens' negotiation list. He reported to Canadiens at St. Hyacinth [sic] that fall and became an instant sensation, though plagued with injuries in his first two seasons. Elmer survived two serious operations that would have forced the average athlete into retirement. He*

---

22 This appears to be T.P.'s first use of Les Canadiens' common label that has prevailed ever since, shortened to "The Habs."

> *did not originally cost Canadiens one dollar, although he subsequently knocked down big dollars as an all-star playing centre ice, one of the finest ever produced. Lach even offered to pay for his own little share of lunch on that eventful day. We never did sign Larson.*

Lach went on to one of the most brilliant careers the NHL has ever seen, and he was one of the pillars in that rebuilding. He was a member of the famous Punch Line with Maurice Richard and Toe Blake. Had he not been standing in the lobby of the Queen's Hotel when T.P. was beginning negotiations with Norm Larson, who knows where he might have ended up, and where the Canadiens might have been without his extraordinary skills.

Toe Blake and Elmer Lach made a pretty good starting point for rebuilding a team. But the famous Punch Line was not completed until the third member of the unit appeared on the scene. That player would become one of the greatest, and perhaps the most exciting, hockey player of all-time, the fabulous Maurice 'The Rocket' Richard. Gorman remembers seeing Richard for the first time, and signing him to his first professional contract.

> *It was modest little Arthur Therien, then coach of the Verdun club, who really brought Maurice Richard under the hockey limelight. In the fall of 1941, Art came into the Forum one gloomy afternoon and remarked "There's a good hockey prospect out at Bordeaux by the name of Maurice Richard. We ought to go out and see him some night. He is big and strong and can really shoot." Two evenings later we drove out to Bordeaux and interviewed Richard. Subsequently he came into Montreal and we quickly signed him to a contract with Canadiens in the*

Quebec Senior Group. He was handicapped through injuries in the seasons of 1942 and 1943 and it was not until 1944 that he blossomed out so brilliantly. In that remarkable 1944 season, Richard established the holy grail of all hockey records when he scored 50 goals in 50 games.

The Rocket.

Richard's first contract with Canadien Seniors was for about $800 for the season. I told a group of Toronto sports writers that winter that Richard would develop into one of the most valuable forwards of all time. What a hearty laugh they all gave me in the press room at Maple Leaf Gardens! I wasn't far wrong in that *prediction. When in command of Les Canadiens I used to slip him $100 every time we beat the Leafs on their own ice. In the 1946 season I had to hand over $500! Richard signed his first contract for me in the Forum office in the fall of 1941. Signing him for Les Canadiens did not cost the club one dollar.*

Incroyable, really.

That trio –Blake, Lach and Richard: the famous Punch Line – scored an even 100 goals among them in a 50-game season in 1943-44, thus putting T.P. Gorman's name on the Stanley Cup for the sixth time. The rebuilding was clearly a huge success already, but there was more to come.

Kenny Mosdell and Jimmie Peters arrived in a most unusual manner. Both were in the armed forces, but they were on a special Reserve List – potential players who were in the services. The question arose in 1945 as to whether these players could be drafted. There was a meeting of the NHL in Montreal in July, 1945 and

after lengthy discussion it was decided that they could be drafted for $5,000 cash. Canadiens, much to the surprise of everyone, drafted Mosdell and Peters. Mosdell was in the Royal Canadian Air Force and Peters was an infantryman in France. "They are off their rockers!" said Art Ross. "Gorman has just thrown away $5,000 on a man who is actually in the trenches."

However, Peters was not on the firing line very long. He and Kenny Reardon were brought back from France and they were soon very important cogs in the Canadiens machine. Kenny Mosdell became equally valuable and was for many years one of the strongest of *the forwards. Dick Irvin's club came back with a rush to win the Stanley Cup, eliminating Boston Bruins in the finals. Mosdell and Peters proved two of the finest players ever drafted. At $5,000 each they were certainly bargains. They were young and strong and fitted into the Canadiens' attack perfectly. Les Canadiens never regretted handing the NHL that cheque for $10,000.*

Add in some young but mighty impressive hockey talent – names like Emile 'Butch' Bouchard, Bill Durnan, Gerry McNeil, Floyd 'Busher' Curry, Doug Harvey – and a great coach like Dick Irvin, and the result became entirely predictable. Les Canadiens won the Stanley Cup again in the 1945-46 season.

That Cup was T.P.'s seventh – and last – Stanley Cup.

T.P., front row right, and Dick Irvin, front row left, with their 1946 cup-winning Montreal Canadiens.

SOME OF THE GREAT ONES

With seven Stanley Cups under his belt, and a couple of near-misses, Tommy Gorman had coached, managed and witnessed some of the greatest hockey players to play the game in the first half of the twentieth century. He put Frank Nighbor at the top of his list, but there were several others about whom he writes fondly.

> *Lionel Conacher was, without doubt, the greatest all-around athlete I have ever handled. Frank Nighbor was tops among the hockey forwards with Maurice Richard a close second and Eddie Gerard was my most valuable defenceman. For goalkeepers this is difficult. I had some marvelous net guardians, including Alex Connell, Chuck Gardiner, Bill Durnan and Roy Worters. Connell had six straight shut-outs and he gave the greatest goalkeeping display on record when Maroons defeated Leafs in the second Stanley Cup game at Toronto in 1935; Gardiner won the Stanley Cup with a magnificent exhibition against Detroit at Chicago in 1934 and Bill Durnan carried off the Vezina Trophy six or seven times. As for Worters, I still think he was the greatest of all. Maybe*

> *I'm prejudiced, but I always loved that little guy from Toronto. George Boucher was the finest stickhandler hockey has ever developed and Jack Darragh the most versatile as he could perform with equal effectiveness at center, right wing or left wing. Dick Irvin was my greatest coach and Bill O'Brien my finest trainer. Dave Trottier stood out as my finest skater.*

Tommy considers many others with whom he crossed paths.

> *My best purchase in hockey? Without hesitation I would say it was Leroy Goldsworthy. I scouted him in London and bought him for $3,000 for the Black Hawks. 'Goldie' played grand hockey in the latter stages of the championship race; in each and every game he proved a stand-out. He was fast and strong, with a beautiful rising shot; he back-checked effectively and proved in every way a great asset.*

> *My greatest trade? When I landed Lionel Conacher from the Montreal Maroons for Teddy Graham, who had starred on the Chicago defence. The best back-checker? Lolo Couture, who played right wing for the Chicago Black Hawks. Time after time when a goal against Chuck Gardiner would appear a certainty, his slim figure would suddenly appear out of nowhere to take the on-rushing puck carrier out of the play. Other terrific back-checkers I handled included Frank Nighbor, Jimmie Ward, Gus Marker and Elmer Lach. As a fore-checker, Lach was in a class by himself.*

T.P. had a special fondness for Sprague Cleghorn.

He was the cheapest player I ever landed, one of the greatest, a real superman if ever there was one. In the summer of 1918 Sprague broke one of his ankles in a fall at home. He sneaked out of Notre Dame Hospital in the dead of night, slipped on St. James Street and broke the other foot. The Wanderers placed him on the retired list. Sprague asked Ottawa Senators to give him a chance. I asked Sam Lichtenheim if we could have him. "Yes, with my compliments" replied Mr. Lichtenheim, "but remember, he has two broken feet."

So Sprague became a Senator. Two weeks later he called up to report.

"Send me two first-class tickets from Montreal to Ottawa" he requested. Those tickets cost the Senators $7.50. And what a star he became. He figured on two Stanley Cup teams with the Senators and then one for Les Canadiens. He was fast and strong, with the heart of a lion and he had a terrific shot. For two one-way tickets from Montreal to Ottawa, Sprague Cleghorn proved a pretty good bargain.

Then there was R.J (Hooley) Smith,

one of the finest players I ever signed. I finally secured his signature on a contract in 1924 and he proved a star from the first night he stepped out on the Auditorium ice. He signed a three-year contract at $3,000 per season and did not receive a dollar for signing. Frank Ahearn subsequently sold Hooley to Montreal Maroons for $25,000. At that, the Maroons secured a genuine bargain.

Still in the category of 'The Greatest', Tommy recalls his four greatest lines: Nighbor, Broadbent and Denenny; Lach, Blake and Richard; Romnes, March and Thompson; Smith, Ward and Northcott. Regarding teams, TP recalls that

> *the strongest team we ever produced for Quebec League competition was that coached by 'Turk' Broda*[23] *in the season of 1953-54. It consisted of Ray Frederick in the nets with Bobby Copp, Frank Stahan, Gordie Johnson, Johnny Arundel and Bobby Robertson on defence.*[24] *The number one line was made up of Dusty Blair, Leo Gravelle and Howard Riopelle and the second by Emile Dagenais, Jack Giesebrecht and Allan Kuntz. For the third attack we had Bep Guidolin, Red Johnson and Jerry Foley. Riopelle carried off the scoring honours while Leo Gravelle led the league in goals scored.*
>
> *The most powerful six man team ever produced in Stanley Cup play consisted of Clint Benedict in goal, Sprague Cleghorn and Eddie Gerard on defence, Frank Nighbor at center, Harry Broadbent at right wing and Cy Denenny at left wing.*

Of course, he didn't catch all the fish in the pond. Fate intervened several times, most notably in the sad case of Nels Crutchfield, a superbly-talented player out of McGill University in Montreal.

> *I saw enough of Nels Crutchfield in 1935 to realize that he would be one of the greatest – probably the greatest*

---

23 Walter Edward Broda acquired the nickname 'Turkey Egg' in school, because he was freckled. The name became shortened to 'Turk' and stuck.

24 Regarding the player position in hockey, 'defence' is the Canadian spelling; 'defense' is the American spelling.

> *– hockey star of all time. In every department, Nels was positively wonderful. However he was almost fatally injured that summer in a car accident, suffering a brain concussion which left him lingering for many weeks between life and death. Surgeons told him he could never play hockey again.*

And he never did, ending the promising career of a man most modern hockey enthusiasts have never heard of, but who was destined, in Gorman's eyes, to become one of the finest players ever.

Much earlier in his career, Gorman lost out on signing a player who went on to become one of the best left wingers ever, Aurel Joliat. It was 1921 and Gorman, in addition to his duties with the Ottawa Senators, was still the sports editor of the *Ottawa Citizen*. George 'Buck' Boucher came into the office one morning and informed Gorman that there was a kid down on the Ottawa River "who could skate like the wind and handle a stick like a champion. He is going to be a super star." That kid was Aurel Joliat. Tommy didn't waste any time going after the kid.

> *We offered him a contract and Aurel appeared anxious to play hockey in Ottawa. Then we hit a snag. Joliat had practiced several times with the Ottawa Rough Riders football team, and unfortunately the Big Four Rugby Union rules were very strict. If Joliat signed a professional hockey contract, he could not play interprovincial football. What a barrier!*
>
> *That night Joliat caught a trans-continental train headed for Regina, being dissatisfied with the terms offered by the Rough Riders. Soon he joined the Saskatoon hockey club in the Western League and accordingly, Ottawa lost all claim to Joliat. Just one year later, Leo Dandurand*

> *in Montreal carried out one of his finest trades, sending 'Newsy' Lalonde to Saskatoon in exchange for Joliat who proceeded to scale the championship heights with Les Canadiens. Had it not been for the Rough Riders and football league rules at the time, Joliat would have carried out his brilliant career with the Senators.*

So this perpetual man in motion, T.P. Gorman, had to surrender to the fickle finger of fate on more than one occasion, but as Lionel Conacher once told him, "Gorman, you lucky Irishman, if you fell into a frog pond you would come up covered with gold!"

KEEP THE PUCK OUT OF YOUR NET!

Tommy Gorman had some sensational goal-scorers play for him. He had some exceptional defencemen on his teams. Yet to him, the most important player on the team was his goalkeeper.

> *When our Black Hawks carried off their first Stanley Cup in 1934, goaltender 'Chuck' Gardiner proved our biggest hero. Ottawa Senators back in 1921 defeated Edmonton for the Stanley Cup thanks to the phenomenal goaltending of lanky Clint Benedict. When our Maroons in 1935 eliminated Chicago Alex Connell gave a magnificent display of goaltending. Les Canadiens under Dick Irvin played to capacity houses but did not achieve much success on the ice until 1943 when we signed Bill Durnan. Frank Brimsek helped win two Cups for the Bruins. When "Turk" Broda was at his best Toronto Maple Leafs proved invincible. Roy Worters, who played in Pittsburg and with the New York Americans, was the only man who completely mastered the trick of deflecting*

shots to the side. He could do so with his gloves or his pads. I still think he was the greatest of all.

Roy Worters.

If T.P's hockey philosophy was that goalkeeping was the essential component, he was also of the view that money alone couldn't buy a good player.

> *You cannot place the long green stuff at right or left wing, you cannot make it back-check. Smart hockey operators will not sell you valuable puck-chasing material. In all my hockey career I was not able to secure through the flash of money, players who really proved valuable. There are actually three ways of securing good players. They must be developed, drafted or landed in trade. The powerful Cup team which we produced for Les*

> *Canadiens in 1946 cost the Canadian Arena Company practically nothing. We developed or traded for players like Bill Durnan, Butch Bouchard, Maurice Richard, Glen Harmon, Ken Reardon, Elmer Lach and others.*

Gorman was not alone with this philosophy.

> *Connie Smythe did a marvelous job for the New York Rangers. Every season Jack Adams in Detroit has come up with a powerful club. Terry Sawchuck, Gordie Howe and Ted Lindsay were his most sensational finds. On my own list of discoveries, I must place Rocket Richard at the top.*

Tommy reflects on his time with the great Richard.

> *During the five seasons in which I managed 'Rocket' Richard, we never had the slightest bit of difficulty. He seldom received a penalty and never got into trouble with either Frank Calder or Mervin Dutton, then presidents of the NHL. We managed to keep him cool and collected. Toe Blake, for instance, had a tremendous influence over the flaming Rocket. He would frequently call me aside and say "Richard is in a bad humour. You better have a talk with him." I used to emphasize the fact that the officials were bosses and repeatedly cautioned Richard about talking back to the whistle tooters, which he seldom did. He was subject to a great deal of heavy checking and after he established himself as a truly great forward opposing teams always called upon their hottest checker to trail him. Had it not been for Blake and a couple of others Richard might have had more serious troubles.*

> *In my last season with Les Canadiens I promised the Rocket that I would slip him $100 cash for each game the Habitants won on Toronto ice. He proved terrific that winter and helped Canadiens carry off all five matches in Maple Leaf Gardens. Richard collected his $500 and smiled widely. "Too bad we didn't make it $1,000. I would have been rich!" For a youngster who we picked up from an open air rink at Bordeaux, Maurice has not done badly*

writes Gorman, in a rather large understatement.

THE HIGH COST OF HOCKEY

If hockey was set to move into the big time in North American sports, so too were the costs. Or, so thought T.P. In the context of the times, hockey probably was an expensive adventure for the backers of the sport. In to-day's hockey world with its multi-million dollar player salaries, billionaire owners and single franchises worth in excess of a billion dollars, the money fretted over by T.P. and his confreres is laughable. Looking back from his desk in 1957, Tommy writes about the high cost of keeping a team in business.

> *On occasions of the Ottawa Senator jaunts to Montreal in the palmy days of the all-Canadian NHL our meal expense for the entire team came to $22.00. On recent trips of the modern Senators the dinner cheque was usually $100. We used to get steaks for $1.15. They now cost approximately $4.50. Skates come to about $60 per pair and hockey sticks are $3. In the Quebec League in their last season the Ottawa club handed over $25,000*

to railroad and bus companies. Clubs had to take in at least $150,000 to break even. It couldn't be done.

T.P. marvels at the way salaries were jumping.

During the First World War when he served in the Air Force, the Ottawa Hockey Association signed Frank Nighbor, who was then stationed at Toronto, at $600 for the season. He would make special trips to Ottawa for the games. 'King' Clancy's original contract was for $1,300, with play-off bonuses and some of the Ottawa regulars, even in the boom days when they captured the Stanley Cup, received approximately $2,000. Hooley Smith signed a three-year contract at $3,000 per season and Sprague Cleghorn, one of the greatest defencemen of all time, drew down the princely sum of $100 per week with his apartment rent extra.

Of course, when United States clubs entered, up jumped the salaries. Eddie Shore sometimes collected $20,000, it is reported, from the Boston Bruins. Howie Morenz was always treated in a most generous manner by Les Canadiens and Charlie Conacher rated among the top men when playing for the Toronto Leafs. Billy Burch signed a three-year contract with the New York Americans at $7,000 per season and Lionel Conacher at $6,000 per season. The minimum in the NHL now[25] *is $7,500 and some of the powerful drawing cards knock down $20,000, plus bonuses. Jean Beliveau and Maurice Richard are in this class.*

25 1957

Then there was the not-so-small matter of franchise fees.

> *Frank Ahearn was another who fought strenuously against the admittance of United States clubs to the National Hockey League. He figured, and rightly so, that Thomas Duggan slipped it all over Frank Calder and the NHL directors when he received franchises for Boston and New York for $5,000 each; also that Chicago, Detroit and Rangers secured land-office bargains when they crashed into the big pro circuit for $50,000 each. "Duggan should have been charged $50,000 for his franchises and the clubs which followed him in should have been charged $200,000 each" Mr. Ahearn was quoted as saying.*
>
> *Subsequent events proved that the Ottawa magnate was correct. Hockey has been a terrific money-maker for Boston, New York, Chicago and Detroit. The original NHL clubs, Canadiens, Ottawa, Quebec and then Toronto did not pay anything for their operating rights, while Hamilton Tigers were admitted for $10,000. Bill Dwyer on one occasion when heavily in the chips turned down $350,000 cold cash for the New York Americans and Major Fred McLaughlin really laughed out loud when a Chicago group offered him $200,000 for the Black Hawks.*

To think that Las Vegas interests in 2016 paid $500 million for a franchise. How times have changed.

HOME SWEET HOME

T.P. Gorman's work-a-day world took him all over North America, bringing him into contact with famous Hollywood stars and Chicago and New York gangsters, the best hockey players in the world and some of the greatest entertainers, the rich and famous, and the not-so-rich and not-so-famous. But Ottawa was home, and the chance to operate his own arena, his own racetrack, his own baseball team proved an irresistible lure.

Gorman left Montreal following the 1946 Canadiens' Stanley Cup win and headed to the national capital where, at the age of 60 and at a time when many with less energy were contemplating retirement he embarked on the next phase of his remarkable life. He bought the Ottawa Auditorium; he owned the Ottawa Senators of the Quebec Senior Hockey League; he owned the Ottawa Nationals baseball club; and by 1952 he had acquired Connaught Park Racetrack. He owned a home at 314 Clemow Avenue in the Glebe, one of the city's more prominent and attractive streets. It was a lovely area, within easy walking distance of the Auditorium and of Lansdowne Park, home of the Nationals. Connaught Park was just a 15-minute drive away on the Quebec side of the wide, fast-flowing Ottawa River.

T.P.'s 1948–49 Ottawa Senators of the Quebec Senior Hockey League won the Allan Cup that season.

It must have seemed a million miles away from the excitement of New York, Chicago, Montreal, and Tijuana. Ottawa had barely 200,000 residents at the time, and was a sleepy civil service town where businesses relied almost totally on the twice-monthly civil service payroll to keep afloat. It was a tough town in which to launch any business, let alone a number of sporting businesses. But Tay Pay was not deterred either by age or by the potential for financial disaster.

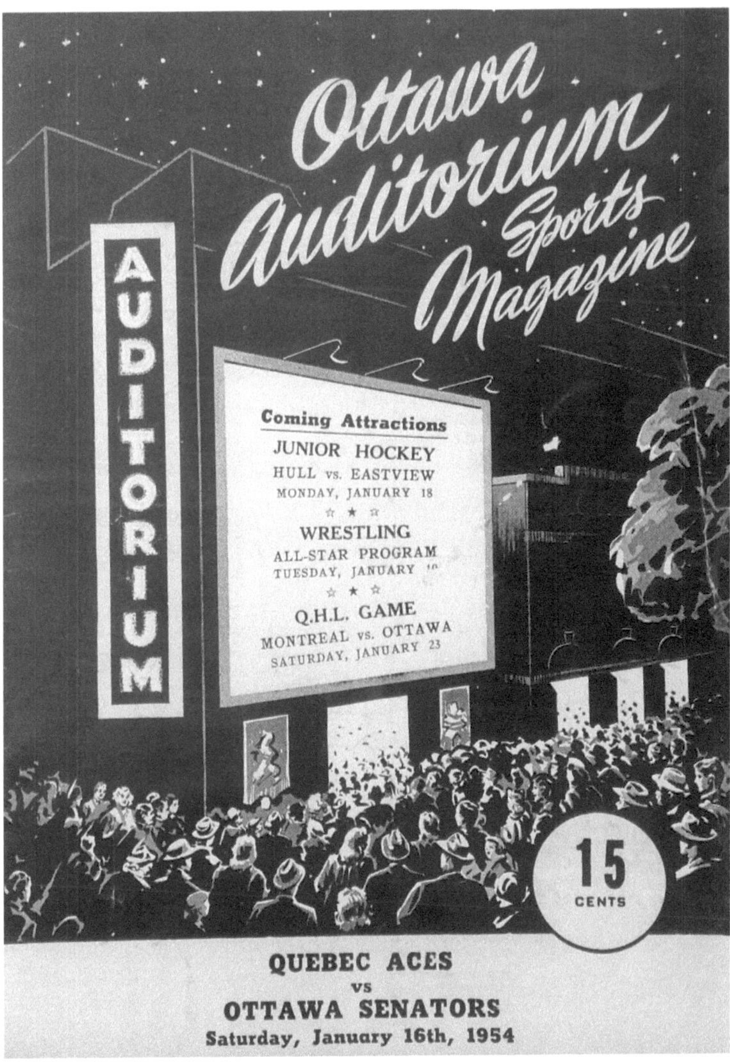

He loved Connaught Park, with which he had been involved for many years, partnering with Leo Dandurand and Joe Cattaranich in the 1930s and '40s and assuming sole ownership by 1952.

Watching the morning workouts.

> *Connaught Park was launched in 1910, financed through public subscription in 1911 and 1912 and opened in 1913. Bookmakers originally operated at the Aylmer Road plant, but pari-mutuels were introduced in 1920. On Labor Day of that year over $200,000 passed through the pari-mutuel machines there. Much of the first issue of Connaught Park stock was bought up by New York and Buffalo interests. The great Discovery ran his first race there as a two year-old and the Duke of Connaught presented a silver trophy to the Jockey Club. Princess Patricia attended the first running for her father's silverware.*[26]

Connaught Park was built as a thoroughbred track, a one-mile oval in front of a grandstand which could hold about 3,500 customers and there was stabling on the backstretch for 500 horses. In those days race meetings were very short – 7 to 14 days – and track operators had to race under federal charters which generally allowed a maximum 14

26 Princess Patricia of Connaught (1886-1974) was a granddaughter of Queen Victoria.

days of action per year. Horsemen were a hardy lot. They were forever packing their tack, and their horses, and moving to the next stop on the circuit, often by train.

When Gorman took over Connaught Park in 1952 thoroughbred racing was strictly a daytime affair. In a small city like Ottawa-Hull, where nearly everyone, it seemed, was a civil servant toiling away in some rather dreary wartime building, afternoon crowds were hard to come by. Therefore, in 1955 he embarked on an expensive, risky adventure. He had a half-mile track cut into the infield , utilizing the home stretch of the existing one-mile track, and, to the amazement of the horse racing world, he put in lights so that he could offer the first night-time thoroughbred racing in North America.

That experiment did not last long. Only a few days after the start of the race meeting the heavens opened up, the race track became a sea of slop, and the jockeys refused to ride on the new half-miler. Exit thoroughbred racing. Enter harness racing. Gorman suggested the thoroughbred set get out of town, pronto, and within a short time he had put together a race meeting for the Standardbreds. Writing a couple of years later, TP reflects:

> *One of the most amazing developments in sport in Canada concerns the remarkable success within the last couple of years, of harness racing. During the past summer*[27] *at Blue Bonnets and Richelieu Park in Montreal they handled over $60 million through the pari-mutuel machines. During the last summers in which thoroughbred racing was conducted at Blue Bonnets and Connaught Park they did remarkably well, but horse owners cooked their own geese, so to*

---

27 1957

speak, when they held up the clubs for purses which they could not possibly afford. Consequently Connaught Park and Blue Bonnets transferred to the Standardbreds, with results that have become very satisfactory. All the Quebec clubs will show handsome profits on their 1957 operations and it is quite obvious that the harness boom will continue indefinitely.

The original Connaught Park, just as the harness racing boom began.

Connaught Park, like so many other North American tracks, rode the harness racing boom to unprecedented heights of popularity, and Gorman had been in on the ground floor. When he died in 1961, the game was really beginning to take off, so he missed out on the big pay day but it was his fine-tuned sense of timing and his incredible promotional abilities that enabled the Standardbreds to gain a strong foothold in the Ottawa-Hull sporting scene. His efforts there, and in other racing ventures in Montreal, enabled his induction to the Canadian Horse Racing Hall of Fame.

SOME WINNERS – AND A LOSER

Sometimes you win, sometimes you lose. That's true in sports, it's true in the entertainment business and it certainly was true for Tommy Gorman as a promoter. He ran hockey teams, of course, and baseball teams and race tracks. He was an amazing publicist and promoter for all of those ventures. He was great newspaper copy wherever he went.

There was, as well, still more on his plate – wrestling, concerts, rodeos, circuses, evangelists – and he worked with some of North America's best-known entertainers. Wrestlers drew some of the Ottawa Auditorium's largest crowds in the early 1950s. Ottawans packed the building to see the likes of Gene Kiniski, Yukon Eric, Yvon Robert, The Great Togo, The Mills Brothers, Argentine Rocca, Little Beaver and Sky Low Low, to mention just a few. These guys were household names across North America and Gorman reveled in their company. He worked closely with wrestling promoters Eddie Quinn in Montreal and Frank Tunney in Toronto to put together top-flight entertainment for the good citizens of Bytown.[28] Curiously, after waging ferocious

---

28 Ottawa's earlier name.

battles in the ring, several of the combatants would pile into the same automobile for the drive back to Montreal headquarters!

The Mills Brothers.

Tay Pay worked with Larry Sunbrock, probably the greatest rodeo promoter of all time, in Montreal and Ottawa.

> *In 1944 Larry Sunbrock offered his Rodeo and Wild West Show to us at the Forum. He proposed a 50-50 split with the Forum but demanded a $2,000 guarantee. "Might as well toss that $2,000 out the window" commented one Forum official as he countersigned Larry's cheque. Well, the rodeo grossed over $140,000 and we handed the Forum a profit of $50,000 for a 10-day show.*

Later, Sunbrock and his entourage came to Ottawa to play the Auditorium, at a time when the old cross-town railroad tracks ran right beside the Auditorium. Shows of this kind often arrived by rail, and parked at a siding across from the Aud. Sensing an opportunity to garner a little extra publicity, Sunbrock had one of the cowboys release a couple of rodeo bulls into the streets near the Aud, resulting in a merry chase which received widespread media coverage – and everybody in town knew the rodeo had arrived. The Ottawa police were not amused.

> *They laid a charge against Larry for holding a street parade without a permit. He answered the summons all right, but took all his cowboys and cowgirls on horseback up to the police station. The Ottawa police were glad to see the last of Larry Sunbrock.*

There was Margaret Truman, daughter of U.S. President Harry S. Truman, who came to Ottawa to sing in aid of the victims of a recent Greek disaster. She insisted on paying all her own expenses from and back to New York and she appeared in a wonderful song recital at the Auditorium. Her musical career was brief; she went on to become a popular mystery writer with Washington, DC, the back-drop for many of her stories.

One time Gorman brought Roy Rogers and The Lone Ranger to the Forum in Montreal to star in a spectacular attraction as part of the Wild West Rodeo. As a grand finale it was decided that Roy and the Lone Ranger would ride around the sawdust ring shaking hands with as many people as possible.

> *And then, horror of horrors, we discovered that the Lone Ranger had never been on a horse. He, who had ridden the cold and hot prairies in merciless pursuit of hundreds*

> *of hardened bad men, hadn't even felt the thrill of a saddle beneath him. However, we soon located a nice, peaceful gelding and, after Roy Rogers had given him a few lessons, behind closed doors of course, The Lone Ranger consented to the proposed dramatic conclusion. And as thousands of men, women and children at each performance cheered enthusiastically within that jam-packed Forum, my heart went bumpety bump. I was afraid the fabulous Lone Ranger would fall off his horse!*

There was the night in November, 1944, when Gorman took a virtually unknown singer out to a small suburban Montreal nightclub following the singer's appearance at The Forum.

> *They heard a good little floor show and the Master of Ceremonies invited people in his small audience to participate in his program. One slim young man, after continuous persuasion on the part of his lady friend, moved slowly up to the orchestra and inquired if they had the music for 'Embraceable You.' Then he advanced to the microphone and sang the popular number. "This guy is not bad" the club manager whispered. "Do you think I could engage him for a week or two?" "You might," I admitted, "but his price might be high." The unknown singer was Frank Sinatra.*

It wasn't Gorman's only encounter with the man who became one of the greatest entertainers ever. Following one such concert, Sinatra wrote to T.P.:

Dear Tom.

I would like to send several thousand people up to Canada to take Hospitality Lessons from you. Your friendly cooperation during my recent trip will be entered in my book under the Chapter headed 'Heartwarming Experience.' I have been trying to express my reaction to the Dominion musically, but try as I will I can't seem to do a very good job of singing on either 'Maple Leaf Rag' or 'Canadian Capers.' With the whiskey I brought back, I'm doing better. With some of it, I have been drinking a few retrospective toasts to you and yours.

Here's to us having a quick 'next time around.'

Cordially,
Frankie

In 1944 Sinatra commanded a fee of $10,000 for his Forum show, too much for the Forum directors to swallow, so Gorman underwrote the show himself. With ancillary expenses Gorman was on the hook for close to $15,000. A full house attended, the gate was $20,000 and Gorman made about $5,000 on the gig. That was a good chunk of change then. They worked together several times after that – Sinatra's letter is dated in July, 1949 – and one suspects that there was more than one bottle of whiskey drained while Frankie charmed audiences everywhere with his incredible talent.

"Dear Tom, one of the finest men I know, from his friend Frank Sinatra" reads the inscription on this 1948 photo.

If T.P. made money on his first Sinatra promotion, he took a serious bath when he thought the wildly popular evangelist Aimée Semple McPherson would sell out the Forum.

> *Out in Los Angeles Aimée and her religious followers had erected a magnificent temple that glistened like gold under the hot California sun. To it, Aimée had attracted thousands. In her flowing robes of white and blue, with her black bible pressed to her heart, Aimée presented a really gorgeous picture. She possessed a melodious voice and she could certainly toss around that threat of fire*

and brimstone. In her many one night stands Aimée had played and prayed to standing-room only audiences.

Then came that night for her long-awaited appearance in the Montreal Forum. She had visualized hundreds tripping down the carpeted aisles to repent and to receive her blessing, but when the curtain finally went up, Aimée received a terrific shock. The building was practically empty. "Your publicity was good and my show would have been great" explained the disappointed California evangelist. "But no one in Montreal wanted to be saved."

CANADA'S SWEETHEART

There was no television back in 1948, and no way to see, except first-hand, the brilliant figure skating of Ottawa's Barbara Ann Scott. But through the printed word, and word-of-mouth, the diminutive 20-year-old blonde became a Canadian sporting icon. T.P., promoter extraordinaire that he was, sensed an opportunity, and together they embarked on a wild, wacky and altogether wonderful tour of Canada, showcasing Barbara Ann's exquisite Olympic Gold Medal talents in fifty Canadian (and a couple of American) cities and towns.

Competitive skating was a little different back then. A skater actually had to trace figures on the ice as well as present a free-skating program. No female in the world did it better than Barbara Ann. She went to the St. Moritz Olympic Games in 1948 representing Canada, and she came home with Olympic Gold. A monumental achievement, to be sure, but look at what else she accomplished : four-time Canadian champion, European champion, Olympic Gold medalist, Canadian Newsmaker of the Year in 1947, subject of cover stories in Time magazine (1948) and Life magazine (1952), inductee into numerous Halls of Fame, Officer of The Order of Canada, Member of The Order of Ontario, holder of several film credits, and, later, an accomplished equestrienne. It was the Gold Medal, however, which catapulted her into becoming a Canadian icon. Even today, almost seventy years later, her name is synonymous with figure skating in Canada.

T.P. came to know her in a rather convoluted way. During World War II Tommy was busy assembling a powerhouse hockey team in Montreal, much to the chagrin of some opposing general managers who could not figure out how he obtained draft deferrals for some players, and exit permits for others who were already overseas. NHL President Frank Calder had assigned him the difficult task of securing what Calder called 'the green light' from the army. Tommy was having a great deal of difficulty getting a meeting with the Minister of Defense, the Hon. Col. Layton Ralston. But on Ralston's staff was the former mayor of Westmount, a man well known to T.P, one Brigadier 'Jimmie' de la Lante. The Brigadier introduced Tommy to Colonel Clyde Scott who helped pave the way for a meeting with the Minister. Tommy writes:

> *Clyde Scott died with startling suddenness shortly, leaving his widow Mary and little Barbara Ann. I can still visualize Clyde Scott, sitting in on that all-important interview with the Minister of Defense. As we separated I remarked "Col. Scott, I hope I shall someday have the opportunity of reciprocating." "Possibly for Mary or Barbara Ann" he said. "Please remember, they mean everything to me." During the memorable tour of Skating Sensations in 1949-50, I often thought kindly of Clyde Scott. He would have been extremely proud of Barbara Ann.*

When Tommy acquired the Ottawa Auditorium in 1948, the famed Minto Skating Club of Ottawa and its annual Minto Follies Ice Show, held at the Aud, were well known to the new owner. After she won the Olympic Gold, Barbara Ann, a Minto Club member, returned to Ottawa and a huge welcome from its adoring citizens. Remember, in those days the Olympics were for amateurs, true amateurs, unlike today, so a decision had to be made by Barbara Ann, stay an amateur, or turn pro and make a little money? By now Tommy was helping to drive this bus,

> *and in 1948 I introduced the fabulous Art Wirtz to Barbara Ann in the Chateau Laurier café. Afterwards he presented his offer to the Olympic champion. He wanted her to take part in his production at The Music Hall in New York City, to groom her for 'Hollywood on Ice'. Barbara Ann was in the hands of an entity called The St. Lawrence Foundation and when Wirtz tabled his offer of $1,000 per week, plus all expenses for her and Mrs. Scott in New York, a Foundation spokesman said "that is just peanuts" to which Wirtz replied "Well, I guess I had better go sell my peanuts." He didn't make another offer.*

Enter MCA, the Music Corporation of America. They had an interest in Barbara Ann and teamed up with the St. Lawrence Foundation to promote the brilliant skater. Apparently, they had no idea how to do it.

> *They had ambitious plans, but they evidently all vanished. True, they did produce Barbara Ann in a skating specialty show at Roxy's Theatre in New York City. This proved a 'five day deal' with which Barbara Ann soon became disgusted. There were trained dogs and*

> *ponies on the same program, the Olympic champion had a little dressing room about five flights up and publicity for that New York engagement seemed awful, just one little three-sheet poster outside the Roxy Theatre which advertised 'Barbara Ann Scott in her professional debut.'*
>
> *What a debut! Barbara Ann literally tossed in the sponge after a few appearances at Roxy's and accepted only a few engagements until the following summer when MCA sent her to Regina for some kind of an industrial exhibition. Mary Scott subsequently informed me that she felt sorry for Barbara Ann on that occasion. A poultry show operated in the same building. Barbara Ann's Regina appearance proved a real turkey, as they say in show business, and it looked like curtains for the diminutive B.A.*

Not quite. Indeed, not ever.

> *In the summer of 1949 we negotiated through MCA and representatives of the St. Lawrence Foundation, offering Barbara Ann a minimum guarantee of $50,000 for a 20-week Canadian tour. We assembled 'Skating Sensations' in the Ottawa Auditorium, with Osborne Colson as director, and completed an itinerary for Barbara Ann's appearance in no fewer than 50 Canadian cities and towns.*

Of course there were skeptics. Some predicted that the show would run into financial ruin and be stranded on the prairies. Others suggested the same result somewhere west of the Rockies. But they were wrong.

> *Backed by one of the most elaborate publicity campaigns ever launched in Canada or the United States, 'Skating Sensations' set out in early October on its lengthy Canadian tour, which was to cover over 12,000 miles, attract over 800,000 people and gross nearly one million dollars.*

The skeptics were astonished. The mathematically inclined reader might quickly realize that the average cost of a ticket to see Skating Sensations and the remarkable Barbara Ann Scott was about $1.00. Most of the 12,000 miles was covered by train and bus. Most of the hotels were two chandeliers shy of the Ritz. None of the arenas resembled today's fantastic ice arenas. It was not an easy tour but "under all these trying circumstances Barbara Ann was most co-operative" remembers T.P.

> *Barbara Ann of course was the magnetic attraction but we had rounded up a terrific show. Our glorified Canadian Glamour Gals left grand impressions everywhere. In one western Canadian city Skating Sensations played five nights to capacity audiences, where a U.S. skating production had recently flopped. Barbara Ann skated remarkably well and received an enthusiastic reception everywhere. It was the most profitable season she ever had, earning $200,000 as her cut from the trip.*

Barbara Ann Scott.

An extraordinary trip like that was not without its issues, though.

> *Winnipeg, where water poured through the roof on our new $100,000 costumes; Vancouver, where handsome police escorted our Glorified Canadian Glamour Gals right home after each performance; New Westminster, where Dr. Tom Rennie offered to fix some of my teeth he had knocked out in a lacrosse game many years ago; Kamloops, where some of the dude ranchers frightened the skaters by shooting off blank cartridges; Kelowna, where they handed out so many British Columbia apples that most of the gals collapsed with tummy aches; Vernon, where enthusiastic fruit magnates burst through the doors after all tickets had been sold; Calgary, where Barbara Ann had to respond to 10 encores after each performance.*

> *And more thoughts from across the west: Edmonton, where we had to give an extra matinee for 11,000 school children and orphans, many of whom were brought into the arena via police and fire wagons; Saskatoon, where one of the union representatives stuck us for $900 which we had previously paid on the Coast; Lethbridge, where civic officials forced us to move all our equipment out into the snow, so dangerously packed was the arena; Medicine Hat where we played a one-night stand practically in darkness because of electrical trouble.*

And then, back into Ontario. It is mid-winter by now, and the troupe is not travelling by luxurious charter jet, remember.

> *Sudbury, where it was 30 below with no heat in the dressing rooms; Sault Ste. Marie, where a devout clergyman invaded Barbara Ann's quarters to read the Bible to Mary Scott; Timmins, where snow actually drifted through our hotel windows in freezing temperatures; Barrie, where we had to live in Pullmans because of hotel repairs; Hamilton, where firemen strolled through the audience and backstage with fire extinguishers because the old rink had been condemned; Niagara Falls, where blushing skaters had to accept accommodation in The Honeymoon Motel.*

By now, ordinary mortals would have been ready to fly the white flag. But no, not this redoubtable gang. Onward they went, to Brantford, Stratford, Kitchener, Oshawa, Cornwall and then to Ottawa, "where Skating Sensations received an immense welcome "writes Tommy. OK. Time to call it quits? Are you kidding?

> *Then the long sleeper jump to the Maritimes; Glace Bay, where huge waves rolled in from the Atlantic, nearly washing the arena away; St. John, where the RCMP arrested one of our chauffeurs because he had a loaded gun; Halifax, where 2,000 sailors from HMS Magnificent roared a wild welcome for Barbara Ann; Charlottetown, where we opened the show at 10:30 p.m. after being stuck in the ice for six hours in the Straits of Northumberland; Stellarton, where miners parked their lights and axes in the lobby. And then westward to Sherbrooke, where we had to use sleighs on account of snowstorms; Rimouski, where we found the finest food in all of Canada; then Valleyfield, Troy and Utica in New York State, Shawinigan Falls and finally Chicoutimi, where many of the skaters broke down and cried, realizing they had reached the end of a 12,000 mile tour.*

But, Rimouski, the finest food in all of Canada? Who knew?

> *Nowhere in Canada were the skaters received so enthusiastically as at Rimouski, Quebec. When the special train rolled into Rimouski there were hundreds out to welcome Miss Scott and all her company. Ideal arrangements had been made at two of the best hotels in Rimouski and plans at the arena could not have been improved upon. Skating Sensations played to three packed houses, there were luncheons and receptions for Barbara Ann and her stars and on our first morning we were shocked to see most of the stars driving around town in autos which had been placed at their disposal. And the food! It was really wonderful. Members of*

> *the company often reminisced at the close of the tour and invariably someone would speak up: Remember Rimouski! It undoubtedly stood out.*

Did we mention food? Of course highly trained athletes have to eat, and eat properly…perhaps a little easier in that era, pre The Golden Arches, Burger King, Taco Bell, KFC et al. But still, twenty weeks on the road made dining a challenge. During the Maritime portion of the tour

> *we ate so much fish it almost became tasteless. Just before the reception at the Lieutenant-Governor's residence in Charlottetown, Barbara Ann remarked "Gosh, I hope they have some steak." Mary Scott added "I would settle for some roast beef. I have almost forgotten what it looks like." And then, as we entered the Governor's palatial home overlooking beautiful Charlottetown Harbour one of his aides rushed up and shook hands warmly. And he said to me "knowing you are an Islander his Excellency has arranged to serve you today some of the finest mackerel that has ever come out of the Atlantic Ocean." Barbara Ann's face grew deathly white!*

Nobody enjoyed pranks, practical jokes and absurd situations more than T.P. He loved to regale his grandchildren with tales of the ridiculous, some of which even had a ring of truth! Herewith, two of his stories from the Skating Sensations tour which are, in all likelihood, true. Recall that on the ferry ride to Charlottetown the ship had become stuck in the ice for six hours.

> *In Amherst a local citizen offered to chauffeur us to Charlottetown and back (via the ferry) for $60. We shook hands on that deal. Someone suggested poker*

> *when the big ferry became marooned in the ice and our chauffeur reluctantly accepted a hand. When we finally reached Prince Edward Island he had all the money. "Where did you round up that chauffeur?" Mrs. Scott angrily inquired. "And incidentally, lend me $20." In Charlottetown someone had discovered that our new chauffeur's room had become loaded with liquor. "I think" volunteered Mrs. Scott, "that you have signed on a bootlegger!"*

Apparently, the ferry ride through the ice to PEI was not a highlight of the trip in Barbara Ann's mom's eyes. T.P. made inquiries back in Nova Scotia to find out more about this chauffer.

> *"Big Pete is all right," one of my friends explained. "But don't play cards with him. He marks 'em all." He was the smartest card manipulator in the Maritimes. He really made a clean-up at the expense of Mrs. Scott and others in our group.*

Tommy was only a partial victim in this case – he hired and paid the guy – but he loved stories like this, even when he was the prime victim. Mrs. Scott, on the other hand, now several weeks into this remarkable journey, had every reason to be a little angry. A little tired maybe, a little frustrated at being stuck in the Straits of Northumberland, certainly tired of fish and probably a little tired of this man in perpetual motion, T.P. Gorman. And, apparently $20 lighter in the pocketbook.

Then there was the stop in Belleville, expected to be a nice, easy small-town stop on the tour. Or not. It seems the building had been oversold by 400 seats.

> *Shorten up the skating area and place chairs on the ice, the arena manager was advised. "Fine, but we have no*

> *chairs" said the increasingly nervous rink boss. "There might be some available at the YMCA." But they had sold all their chairs to the undertaker down the street. So, up from Ottawa we managed to truck 200 chairs but still the situation was desperate. People were battling for tickets. As a last resort we visited that silent funeral parlour. There they were. Three hundred comfortable seats. They had prepared a dear-looking old lady for her last long sleep and there she rested, surrounded by beautiful floral offerings and those 300 seats we needed so badly. Naturally, we extended our deepest condolences. "Poor Aunt Rose" commented one of the teary-eyed relatives. "How we are going to miss her." "Undoubtedly" said our stage manager. "What time is the funeral?" "Three o'clock" they told us. Fortunately the burial service was short and by 3:30 p.m. we had transported all the available folding contraptions to the Belleville arena. Within an hour they were all in place and the rink manager regained his smiling countenance. We never did find out what happened to Aunt Rose.*

And finally, from Down East where the Glamour Girls had to bunk out in a tired old rooming house came a call to T.P. "You had better come and get us out of here" said the caller. "We are in a boot-legger's joint and business is good!"

And so it went on this 12,000 mile odyssey. A million frustrations, a million laughs, a million bucks at the box office, all thanks to a brilliant little skater from Ottawa by the name of Barbara Ann Scott, Canada's Sweetheart.

SONJA – FROM NORWAY WITH LOVE

Sonja Henie's brother Leif, in a book about his sister, wrote that she was obsessed with money and sex, had a vile temper when crossed, and used her family and others shamelessly to advance her own ends. But that, apparently, was not the Sonja Henie with whom T.P. worked during a brief five-week Canadian tour, a tour that came about in 1952 when the gorgeous Norwegian figure skating champion was down and out thanks to some financial and legal problems brought about by her own ill-advised skating tour in the U.S.

Barbara Ann Scott was a great admirer of Ms. Henie's skating ability, and with good reason. The Norwegian was a World Champion for an incredible ten consecutive years, a six-time European champion and an Olympic Gold Medal winner in 1928, 1932 and 1936. Born in 1912 in what is today Oslo, she also excelled at skiing, tennis, swimming and was an accomplished equestrienne. And, she was easy on the eyes.

The money part came later, and in abundance. After the 1936 Olympics Henie turned pro, found her way to Hollywood, and at the peak of her skating and film careers she was reportedly earning $2 million per year, making her one of the world's wealthiest women at that time.

The spectacular Sonja.

Not surprisingly, that volatile combination of incredible athletic talent, Norwegian good looks, a high-spirited personality and a trunkful of money proved rather alluring to a number of men. She married and divorced two men, had affairs with two of her skating partners, and also with boxing legend Joe Louis, famed movie star Tyrone Power and well-known Hollywood actor Van Johnson. She finally settled down near Oslo with Norwegian shipping magnate Niels Onstad, her third husband.

But the girl who came into Tommy's life in 1952 was in some difficulty. She had broken ranks with the Wirtz interests and set out on her own tour, occasionally bumping into Barbara Ann's show and coming out second-best at the box office.

I could never understand what had happened between Sonja and the Norris-Wirtz interests. For many years she had starred at the top of their Hollywood Ice Revue, literally packing them in at New York, Chicago, Detroit and elsewhere. Suddenly she stepped out of the Hollywood presentation and Barbara Ann stepped in. Sonja went on tour with her own show and a bitter rivalry developed. Sonja's tour reached an unfortunate climax in Baltimore when the temporary grandstands collapsed, injuring many and resulting in dozens of damage actions.

They re-organized the Henie spectacle in Boston but skaters discovered, upon their arrival there, that another attraction had been booked into the theatre where they were to have appeared. Sonja and her company were practically stranded in November, 1952, when we took over the revue for a brief Canadian tour. Writs had been issued by the dozens in Baltimore and some of their props and costumes were threatened with seizure at Boston. They were happy indeed when we succeeded in getting all of their magnificent equipment over the line into St. Andrews, NB. Sonja played before big crowds in St. Andrews, St. John, Fredericton and Halifax, after which she received a grand reception in Ottawa, Pembroke and Kingston.

These small Canadian towns might have seemed a long way from the bright lights of Hollywood, New York and Chicago, but they got her back on her feet financially, and she left Canada. In St. Andrews she had told Tommy : "I'm broke, and how. I don't even know what money looks like." Tommy clearly enjoyed his relationship with Sonja.

> *Of all the skaters our little company had handled Sonja Henie proved herself the greatest trouper. And what showmanship! The little Norwegian developed an amazing personality. Nothing appeared to discourage the girl who had electrified the world with her wonderful skating. Things had obviously been pretty rough for little Sonja after her sensational break with Art Wirtz because after she saw the 'Welcome Back Sonja' sign in the Ottawa Auditorium she broke down and cried like a little child. She had a similar reaction to a similar sign in Halifax.*

Sonja had a keen sense of humour too, especially when it came to her ex-husbands.

> *On one occasion in Halifax Sonja came skating to the rinkside and inquired "Are we going to have a good audience tonight, Tommy?" A sell-out and we will in every arena you appear in, I told her. "That's great," commented Sonja "but anytime you need more spectators let me know. Sonja will send for her ex-husbands and fill the place!"*

Still, she frequently warned Tommy, ever the publicist that he was. "Don't talk publicly about Sonja's Divorce Court experiences. It could happen to any good little girl!"

> *"Are you a married man?" Sonja inquired when we met in her suite in New York. "Yes," I replied proudly. "I have*

> *three children and seven grandchildren." "Lord" shouted Miss Henie, "you are practically a bachelor, aren't you?"*

Then there was the morning in Halifax when Sonja came to Tommy and announced:

> *"You and I are going to a Service Station dinner tonight. I think our show is going to be a big hit here." "Listen, Sonja", I said, "a service station is where you go for gas and oil, to get flat tires fixed and your windshield cleaned. You mean a Service Club. That is where men call one another by their first two initials, and then try to manipulate mysterious business deals."*
>
> *There was quite a commotion when we showed up at the service club. They shifted several chairs to make room, and they brought in the extra food. "That was really nice" said Sonja after we returned to the Canadian National hotel. "I made my little speech and you worked in a couple of good plugs for the show. We will sell lots of tickets in this old town." "That's all right "I assured Sonja. "But I have news for you. Because of the miserable maritime fog, the wild moonshine gin they served at the cocktail party, and my own well known and widely publicized publicity, you and I went to the wrong Service Club reception." However, we went to the right one the next night, and sent complimentary tickets to the other organization which we had erroneously invaded, and all was forgiven.*

Again, in Fredericton:

> *There was a chorus girl who threatened to quit because we could not get her accommodation in the leading hotel. "Do what you can for her" pleaded Sonja. "The drummer is in love with her and we really need him."*

Chorus girls were a dime a dozen, apparently but a good drummer was hard to find.

> *The gorgeous Miss Henie, however, revealed one noticeable weakness. She never wished to retire at night. Tense and excited during her performances, she would take one small glass of wine on her return to the hotel and then relax completely. "Don't disappear" Sonja would inevitably shout at the close of her performance. "We are going out to see people!" Sonja finally married an immensely wealthy Norwegian shipping tycoon. No more courts for her. Last year[29] she wired us: "Come over and visit us in Norway. I will send one of my steamboats up to Quebec to meet you."*

Her brother undoubtedly knew more about her than did T.P., but in Tommy's eyes "she was undoubtedly the greatest little trouper we ever travelled with." Sonja Henie died of leukemia in 1969. She was 57 years of age.

---

29 1956

"I HATED THE ICE"

"I hated the ice. I hated the cold, the smell, everything about it. I only did it for the money." Those are the sentiments of Maria Belita Gladys Olive Lyne Jepson-Turner, uttered after her retirement from professional skating in 1956. One can only imagine how she might have felt if her proposed Canadian tour with T.P. had actually happened.

Belita, as she was known professionally, had been put on skates at the ripe old age of two by a domineering mother who wanted her daughter to be a classically-trained dancer. She thought skating would help develop her daughter physically. She represented Britain at the 1936 Olympics. At the age of 12 (yes, twelve) she finished 16th behind Sonja Henie and a raft of others. But she went on to carve out a show-business career that included several movies and tours with the great ice revues of the time, including Ice Capades.

> *Suddenly she split with Ice Capades and returned to Los Angeles where she was in plays and movies with the likes of Charles Laughton, Charles Boyer and others. She was the most versatile creature on this side of the North Pole. Joe Louis and Jack Dempsey declared Belita was the finest of all skaters. In addition, she could sing in English, French and German, she could act, skate, dance and swim. On top of all this, Belita was really beautiful.*

Born in England, young Belita excelled at skating, despite her professed abhorrence of it, and so, in the spring of 1950, Tommy signed her for an all-Canadian tour. Recall, this was not long after the sensational Barbara Ann Scott tour.

> *We had closed with many of the glamour gals from Skating Sensations to supply colourful background, as Barbara Ann had succumbed to the lure of Hollywood. What a magnetic creature she would have been. Belita was to have received $2,000 per week with a percentage of the profits. Unfortunately the Korean War broke out and the proposed coast-to-coast tour had to be deferred because transportation had been limited to actual wartime enterprises. We had closed with 56 arenas. Cancellation of Belita's Canadian appearances proved a really staggering blow. In the parlance of show business, Miss Turner would really have packed' em in.*

A staggering financial blow, yes, and one could only guess what Belita's thoughts would have been had she endured 56 draughty, cold Canadian arenas. But there was a bright side, as there usually was. Writes Tommy, the great impresario:

I was kind of glad that the Korean war had resulted in such prohibitive travelling restrictions because I don't think I could have survived another trans-Canada jaunt with skating mothers. One was enough for any man!

TOMMY GORMAN AND THE BASEBALL YEARS

In the summer of 2016 The Ottawa Champions lived up to their name. They won the Can-Am League championship with a stirring come-from-behind effort in the league final. They represented the umpteenth incarnation of the game in Ottawa.

There is a long history of baseball in the nation's capital, much of it financially disastrous. Ottawa ball fans have proven that they will support a winning, even a competitive team, but they will stay away in droves from losing baseball teams. And there have been many of those over the years. Only Tommy Gorman and the late Howard Darwin, best known as a highly successful Ottawa jeweler and owner of the Junior A Ottawa 67s hockey team, had any success financially, and even that was fleeting.

Ottawa's flirtation with The Great American Pastime began in 1898 when the Rochester, New York, franchise in the Eastern League was transferred to Ottawa. Known as the Ottawa Wanderers, they lasted but one season in their new northern home. Perhaps that was a portent of things to come.

Gorman was a young newspaperman in 1911 when he joined Shag Shaughnessy in the management of the Ottawa Senators Professional Baseball Team. Gorman was a jack-of-all-trades for the team, but the outbreak of World War I forced the club to fold. Later, various teams known as the Senators played in various leagues, but for all intents and purposes there was no baseball of any account in Ottawa until 1947 when Gorman, after leaving the Montreal Canadiens organization, acquired a franchise in the Border League, a minor league if ever there was one, but a pro league just the same. It was designated as a Class C league, seemingly a long way from the Stanley Cup he had won just a year earlier.

This erstwhile league began operations in 1946 at about the same time Gorman was hoisting the Stanley Cup for the seventh time. The league provided professional baseball entertainment for fans in upstate and western New York and in eastern Ontario and southern Quebec. Teams in Kingston, Sherbrooke and Granby represented Canada. But the two Quebec-based teams could not answer the bell for the 1947 season. Ottawa and Geneva, New York, wanted in, and the league brass was only too happy to replace the Sherbrooke and Granby franchises with these promising newcomers. They joined Kingston, Auburn, Watertown and Ogdensburg in the geographically compact league where virtually all travel was by car, easily the least expensive way to move a bunch of athletes and their equipment from one city to the next.

Ever the optimist, Gorman told reporters "I don't know much about baseball, but I think the pro game has a wonderful future here in Ottawa." There he was, the irrepressible promoter always, trying to sell tickets right off the bat. And so began several years of fun and frustration for T.P. as he attempted to establish the game in a city of fewer than 250,000 souls, a city that had never shown any but the mildest interest in the sport.

Much was needed to get the operation up and running. A playing field, a manager and some players were good places to start. None of the above was in place when Gorman acquired the franchise. He quickly named the team The Ottawa Nationals. Lansdowne Park, under the auspices of the Central Canada Exhibition Association (CCEA) was the only place in town with a grandstand and although it was totally unsuitable for baseball, its long, straight grandstand affording poor sightlines for the game, it was the only option.

Gorman held the rights for baseball at Lansdowne but the CCEA was not the most benevolent of landlords. Tommy had to install a lighting system at his own not inconsiderable expense, he had to badger the CCEA to get the field in playing shape with a decent diamond, and he had to pay to have an outfield fence put in place. And yes, he had to buy his own public address system. Today, especially in the United States, cities fall all over themselves to provide their local sports teams with stadiums, parking lots, roads, and all the other amenities, but this was Ottawa, remember, and it was 1947. Things were different then. Even with all of those obstacles, however, Gorman was doing all he could to revive baseball in Ottawa. "This is the best little sports town in North America and a good ball team is just what it needs" he told reporters.

T.P.'s already long and colourful career in the sports world had put him on a first-name basis with the movers and shakers in many sports, baseball included, and he sought the advice of the great New York Yankee catcher Bill Dickey in his search for a manager of his new ball club. "Get Paul Dean" said Dickey, so Tommy embarked on a journey to Little Rock, Arkansas, to find Dean and convince him to come up north to manage a yet-to-be-fleshed-out team in a Class C league. Paul Dean, better known as 'Daffy' Dean, had recently retired as one of baseball's greatest pitchers. Ottawa? Where's that? Border League? What's that? No players?

Gorman's gift of the gab prevailed, and he successfully persuaded Dean to leave Little Rock and come north to manage the Nationals, a team with no players as yet. T.P. seemingly knew every sports reporter in North America, and they flooded him with telegrams advising him how to go about finding guys who could play the game, at least a little bit. It was, after all, Class C ball, not exactly The Bigs. One Montreal writer telegrammed "I know a great outfielder and slugger you should have. He once stole second base with the bases full" as he had fun with Tommy's admitted lack of baseball acumen.

'Daffy' Dean as manager? What a coup! Daffy was twice a 20-game winner in St. Louis, and the brother of Dizzy Dean, one of the great names in baseball at that time. Dizzy and Daffy were household names across America.

> *When we broke the baseball barrier in 1947, and placed a team in the Border League, we decided to get a 'Big Name' as a manager. ... Paul Dean proved a happy choice for he furnished terrific newspaper copy and attracted hundreds to the ball parks. Paul also rounded up a powerful Class C team. During the play-offs, Paul suddenly landed in with the announcement that he had to rush back to Little Rock because of some trouble in his restaurant, The Purple Cow. Paul carried out the disappearing act faster than anyone I have ever known. Within an hour, he and his family had departed.*

Bill Metzig, whom Paul had brought to Ottawa, took command and won the play-offs during which we learned that Dean had shown up at the World Series in New York. Several important managerial jobs were reportedly offered to the mysterious 'Daffy' but none materialized. Next season he wound up with another minor league club in Texas.

We never regretted signing the colourful portion of the famous 'me and Paul' pitching combination which starred for St. Louis in the World Series of 1934. However, when Paul opened up with the Ottawa Nationals we discovered one unusual fact, which few had ever suspected. 'Daffy' could neither read nor write.

Bill Metzig had to scribble out his line-up each day, and Mrs. Dean read the newspaper stories to the famous right-hander who had never seen the inside of a school. When he ought to have been in the halls of learning, in fact he and brother 'Dizzy' were out in the Arkansas fields picking potatoes. "I was the best potato picker in Arkansas" Paul used to say. And later, a great baseball pitcher.

Now, though, Daffy was back in the bushes. The knowledgeable fans in Ogdensburg were really giving it to him one night. The bleachers there were very close to the field and they let Dean have it from the first pitch to the last. "Dean, you're back in the sticks" they would shout, and Paul took it all with good humour. One night though, he couldn't resist giving something back. "Gawd, when I look around and see you stupid-looking yokels ah know ah'm back in the bushes" he exclaimed to the noisy fans of the Ogdensburg Maples.

A team was assembled, of course, and Dean did not stay long, turning the managerial duties over to Bill Metzig. The team was a resounding success on the field. They led the league by 12 ½ games in their inaugural season and they won three pennants in their first four seasons. They led the league in attendance each one of those four years, too. The Gorman magic was still at work, except financially.

Leading the league in attendance did not mean a financial windfall for Gorman and the Nats. An ad in *The Ottawa Citizen* in 1947 made that much clear. Under a banner headline proclaiming Opening Day for the new team were listed "prices $1.10, 80c, 60c, 25c and all kids 25c anywhere when accompanied by an adult." Even 25c was too much for a lot of kids, it seems. They congregated by the dozens outside the outfield fences to get a glimpse of the game through knotholes in Gorman's rather rickety fence. Thus was born the infamous Knothole Gang.

Tommy's Ottawa Nationals. Pete Karpuk is front row, right; Doug Harvey is middle row, third from right; and Bill Metzig is top row, third from right.

There were some great athletes to watch, playing in the colours of the Ottawa Nationals. Doug Harvey, by 1950 already a marvelous hockey player for the Montreal Canadiens, was a terrific right fielder and he swung a heavy bat. He was an original Nat, winning the rookie-of-the-year award in the Border League in 1947 at the age of 22. Doug was a terrific all-around athlete.

Pete Karpuk was a multi-sport talent who played shortstop for the Nationals and made the all-star team. He was perhaps best known for the 'Karpuk Play' in 1951 when he played for the Toronto Argonauts Football Club. During one important game Pete's competitive spirit got the better of him and he came flying off the bench to tackle an opposing player who was headed for a touchdown. Great tackle, Pete but you are not supposed to do that! Karpuk had luckily survived a terrible car accident in 1950 while playing with the Nationals, an accident which killed teammate Bob Larkin as the team was driving back to Ottawa following a game in Watertown. Karpuk and three others were injured.

Pete later worked for Tommy at Connaught Park. Pete died in 1985 at the age of only 58. Doug passed away in 1989 at the age of 64. Great athletes both, terrific athletes for Tommy when they were sober, but neither took care of themselves when their playing days were over. That old demon rum wore them down much too soon.

Trouble was brewing in the Border League in 1950. Attendance in most towns was dropping and some of the finger-pointing was towards Gorman and the Nats. He had put together too strong a team and some league members, particularly Kingston, wanted to revert to a 'school boys' kind of league with only a few pros allowed on each team. Gorman also had issues with the CCEA. Although he bought and paid for the lights at Lansdowne the CCEA management often rented out the field for night-time activities, and they refused to compensate Tommy for the use of his lighting system.

Tommy appealed to George Trautman, then the czar of minor league baseball, for help in keeping the Border League alive. "We're doing alright but the little fellows like Jimmy Doyle in Watertown and those Polish boys in Auburn require some assistance" Gorman pleaded with Trautman. "Impossible," said Trautman. "The minors have to stand on their own two feet." They couldn't, and the league imploded.

Triple "A" baseball.

Gorman was not yet finished with baseball. He knew all the big names in the sport, and he still held the rights to baseball at Lansdowne Park. The New York Giants were looking for a new home for their New Jersey farm team in 1951. Tommy convinced them to bring the team to Ottawa. It was a huge jump from the Class C Border League to Triple

A ball, and the team the Giants put on the field for Ottawa fans was a good one, too good, in fact. One day the parent club, with a young Willy Mays in tow, flew into Ottawa for an exhibition game against their farmhands, the Ottawa Giants. The Ottawa club beat the big-leaguers handily, prompting the Giants to call up several of the best Ottawa players, a practice which has killed more than one minor league ball club, and it killed the Ottawa franchise. Crowds were averaging 2,800 per game, a break-even point for the New Yorkers and in effect giving them a free farm team, until the best Ottawa players went to New York, and the team itself went into a free-fall. They finished at 62-88, some 31 games behind the pennant-winning Montreal Royals. Attendance went into a free-fall too.

The Giants were annoyed about some of the things they had to pay for at Lansdowne – seemingly minor things like rent for office space, and paying for hot water usage. This would never happen elsewhere they said, but the CCEA was adamant. Furthermore, there was a much bigger issue, the lack of Sunday sports in Ottawa. The Giants left town.

Gorman was unhappy, claiming the Giants had never given Ottawa a chance. But he still held the rights to baseball at Lansdowne, so he took himself to Philadelphia where he convinced the great Connie Mack to put a Philly farm club in good old Bytown. Welcome, then, the Ottawa Athletics for the 1952 baseball season. In their three years there, they fielded teams which went 65-85, 71-83 and finally 58-96, losing seasons all. The A's drew over 153,000 fans in their first season but could not generate any enthusiasm among baseball fans in the capital as the losing continued, and they relocated to Columbus, Ohio for the 1955 season. By then, Tommy had lost interest in baseball, and he turned his energy to the growing horse racing business at Connaught Park. His baseball days were over.

With most game tickets selling for less than a dollar and with no outside sources of revenue such as those enjoyed by pro sports today, the wonder is that the players in the Border League were paid at all. The Nats attracted more than 80,000 fans in 1949. Net gate receipts barely exceeded $40,000 for the entire season. There were 27 names on the Nat's payroll that year and together – together! – they earned $24,490.45. That staggering sum included bonuses totaling $5,128.50. Bill Metzig, the manager, was the big winner, collecting a salary of $3,290 and a bonus of $500. Top salary among the players was Pete Karpuk, with $1,679.90 but no bonus money that year. Doug Harvey – the great Doug Harvey, then just coming into his own as one of the top NHL defencemen of all time – earned $775. But he also got a bonus of $925, making him the highest-paid player on the team at $1,700.

OMG! as today's kids might text. The top three baseball salaries in 2016 each – each! – exceeded $30 million. There were 37 major league baseball players who each made $20 million or more in 2016. The Los Angeles Dodgers' total payroll in 2016 exceeded $246 million. That's about 10,000 times as much as the payroll of the 1949 Ottawa Nationals.

All his life, T.P. had been a great supporter of the City of Ottawa, his hometown. He loved the place, and its people. But City Hall was another matter. In his memoirs, writing after the demise of the baseball business and his Ottawa Senators he writes:

> *Sports operations in the various cities mean a great deal to business. ... They were magnetic attractions for Ottawa district people who spent thousands of dollars when they came to the Capital. ... The City Fathers could have helped immensely in both instances. Now they have gone. ... Other cities contributed immensely in finances and energy to retain their major sports attractions. Not Ottawa. Farewell to hockey and baseball.*

Jack Koffman, Sports Editor of the *Ottawa Citizen*, wrote about the travails of running a baseball operation. "When you look back on it, the City Fathers can't take a great deal of pride in their contribution towards keeping Triple-A ball in the Capital. If any person officially connected with the city has gone out of his or her way to give the A's a helping hand we haven't heard of it." Today, of course most cities (but not all) go to extraordinary lengths to assist their major and minor league teams in many sports.

Baseball returned to the capital in 1993, playing out of a terrific new stadium built near Ottawa's railway station and right beside the major cross-town expressway, The Queensway. With Howard Darwin as principal the Ottawa Lynx were born. Darwin paid $5 million for the Triple-A franchise in the International League. The team, an affiliate of the Montreal Expos, led the International League in attendance that year, averaging more than 8,000 fans per game and in 1995 the Lynx won the International League championship. Heady days, indeed.

It was a quick downhill slide from there. The Expos called up all the best players, just as the Giants had done four decades earlier. The team played badly, fans deserted the ball park and after a dismal 55-88 season in 2007 the team was sold for $7 million and moved to Allentown, Pennsylvania. The new owners sued the City of Ottawa for breach of contract. Nothing much had changed, it seemed, from Gorman's baseball days in Ottawa more than half a century earlier.

Hope springs eternal, though, and in 2008 Ottawa had an entry in the Can-Am League, the Ottawa Rapidz. They too were not very good, going 31-63 in their only season before folding and blaming, in part, the City of Ottawa for allowing the ball park to deteriorate, and for selling off most of the parking surrounding the stadium.

In 2010, along came the Ottawa Fat Cats, (a tongue-in-cheek name and one of the best-named teams in all of sports) who played in the

Inter-County League. They drew reasonably well, averaging about 2,400 fans but the travel logistics—all of the other teams were in southern Ontario—forced the team to throw in the towel after the 2012 season.

But the game plays on. In 2015 the Ottawa Champions took the field in the Can-Am League, going 46-50 and attracting some decent crowds, but they missed the play-offs. They returned for the 2016 season, averaged about 2,500 fans per game and won the League championship.

T.P.'s baseball days were indeed fun, frustrating, and a poor financial investment all at the same time. But in the end, maybe only the "fun" part really mattered. He cavorted with some of the greats of baseball: Bill Dickey, Connie Mack, Paul Dean. He probably had a million laughs with Pete Karpuk, Doug Harvey, and truth to tell, he probably enjoyed the thrust and parry of his battles with the City Fathers in Ottawa, and with the CCEA. Not a bad way to travel!

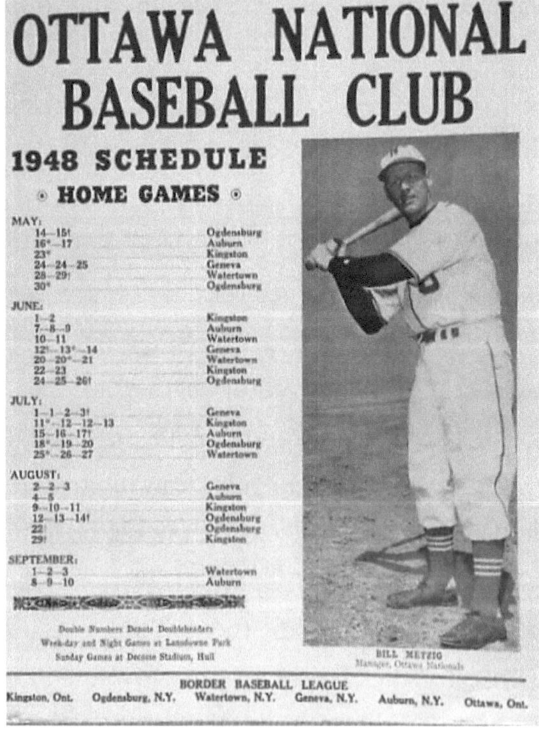

Class C Ball.

MORE FROM THE DIAMOND

A hard-nosed, shrewd, tough negotiator was Tommy Gorman, but he had a remarkable sense of the absurd, a sentimental side, and he loved stories with a slightly salacious bent. Here are three baseball stories, exactly as he writes them in his memoirs. First, the absurd:

> *"Bill Metzig, who piloted Ottawa Nationals in the Border League, couldn't see anything without his glasses. He used to tape them on with adhesive strips. If they slipped out of focus Bill was practically helpless. One night there occurred a brawl in Ogdensburg. Fists flew, boots kicked, and Metzig lost his glasses. There were shouts, screams and groans. Then the police broke it up. When Metzig recovered his spectacles, he discovered he had been pounding the good-looking wife of one of his best friends. "That was the only fight I ever won in the Border League" he afterwards commented.*

And the sentimental:

> *My baseball idol in the early days when I used to slip down to New York to witness games in the American and National Leagues was none other than handsome Hal Chase, brilliant first baseman for the New York Yankees. What a ball player! He could run like a fiend, hammer the ball hard and, around first base, with the big glove on his right hand and his left ready for any emergency, he really scintillated. How he could pull that baseball out of the blue sky, or up out of the dirt! Hal suddenly disappeared from the baseball horizon. Some sort of gambling scandal broke and they claimed the inimitable Hal had been mixed up in it. He appeared to have slipped out of circulation entirely.*
>
> *Back in 1932, we stopped at a gasoline station between San Diego and Los Angeles. There was something familiar about the tall garage operator who came out to supply our needs. When he reached up to haul down the gasoline hose I noticed he was left-handed. "Haven't we met somewhere?" I inquired, still studying the handsome service station attendant, who had noticed the New York plates on our auto. "Possibly," he said with a sad smile and a handshake. "I used to play baseball back east." Yes, he was the magnificent Hal Chase.*

Gorman probably did not know the darker side of Chase's life when he was making those trips to New York. He was just a young man who idolized an athlete, but Chase, whose career lasted from 1905 to 1919, has since been described as "the most notoriously corrupt player in baseball history. He was also, according to many of those who saw him play, the greatest defensive first baseman ever." Chase was implicated in the Black Sox scandal of 1919 and never played in the majors again. He died penniless in California in 1947. Gorman's eye for pure athletic talent was evident though, even as a very young man.

Now, the salacious:

> *Back in the balmy days of the Border League, Harold George of the Chicago Cubs sent us a backstop named Hank. "Boy, how he can hit" commented the affable Mr. George. "Fine catcher too." Hank was a good looker, big and strong, with curly black hair. Socially, as subsequent events proved, he was also tops. Toward the close of the baseball season three ladies came to see me. One was young and pretty as a picture. It was an old, old story. She had come from the east. She and Hank had been keeping company all summer. And she thought I should get out the well-oiled shotgun and read the riot act to Hank. Then she requested a few minutes in private. "Please don't do anything to hurt Hank" she pleaded, tears in her eyes. "I still love the big guy." When I confronted Hank the Hitter he declared "not me," looking as innocent as a little white lamb. "Seven other players on the club, maybe!"*
>
> *Victim #1 departed for her home in the Maritimes. The next week another indignant woman was among my unexpected callers. "One of your ball players has been fooling around with my daughter" she said, "I just want to get my hands on him." Yes, it was Hank the Hitter once again. "What's going on around here?" defended Hank. "I don't even know this baby. They can't pin that on me."*

Victim #3 was the cutest of the trio. She was also the grittiest. My goodness, I said, not Hank the Hitter again! And, sad to relate, it was Hank. This time he was really in for it. "Dad is looking for Hank with a rifle" said the demure-looking Helen. "You better get him out of this town."

In the still of that eventful night, after being politely told by manager Bill Metzig that he had three strikes against him and that Helen's Old Man had been a member of Canada's Bisley Rifle Team, Hank caught a bus to Prescott and slipped quietly into the United States. Several months later he called from Boston. "Tell the fellows I'm going to get married," he said. "It's about time I settled down." What was his batting average? I asked Bill Metzig. "He hit .310 in the Border League and 1.000 with the Ottawa girls" replied Metzig.

GANGSTERS, GAMBLERS AND A RINGER

Horse racing was a vibrant, exciting, rough-and-tumble world in the earlier days of Tommy Gorman's career. It was a world of gangsters, gamblers and the occasional ringer, as WEEKEND magazine headlined in 1957. WEEKEND was a popular Saturday supplement to most of Canada's major newspapers, read by millions across the country each week. In 1957, the magazine ran a major three-part series entitled "Tommy Gorman Remembers" in which the famous sportsman told about some of his most interesting adventures. Not surprisingly, many of the stories came from the world of horse racing.

T.P.'s direct involvement with racing was in an administrative capacity, first in Montreal and then Ottawa, with a spectacular few years in Mexico thrown in. But it was the characters, the shenanigans and the huge money which flew around the game which interested him the most. In his memoirs, and in WEEKEND magazine, he recalls his first year on the job at Connaught Park in what is now Gatineau, Quebec. It was 1920.

What a sucker I must have looked. I became interested in horse racing following World War I, and one of the first things to happen to me was to become the victim of the biggest hoax of the year. A red-haired man from Detroit arrived at Connaught Park, asking for one stall. His horse, he said, was Little Boy. Sure. Glad to give it to him. He entered Little Boy in the fifth race one warm June afternoon and just before they went to the post a ton of 'come back' money flowed into the track, cutting his price from 20-1 to 6-1. Instantly the officials suspected something. "Have the identity of Little Boy established" demanded Judge Nelson, sending for Racing Secretary Joe McLennan. "Hold the horses for 10 minutes."

"That's Little Boy, all right" reported McLennan, one of the keenest of all turf officials. "I'm positive. His markings are unmistakable." Off they went, and Little Boy came down that Connaught Park track with the speed of Man o' War. Jockey Callahan was actually looking back. Then came the wild roar from bookies across the continent. "Seize the horse and arrest his owners" Judge Nelson ordered. We seized Little Boy, but his owners had taken a taxi to Ogdensburg, New York, and were safely across the border. Next morning we turned a heavy hose on Little Boy. His bay coloring disappeared and there stood a magnificent black stallion! "Good Lord!" gasped McLennan. "This is Westy Hogan!" And that's who it was. Westy Hogan, who could probably have beaten any horse in Canada over six furlongs.

Subsequently the entire deception was uncovered. Racketeers had transported Westy Hogan from New Orleans to Detroit. There, a top lady artist in this unusual profession, Ida Richings, had transformed Westy Hogan into Little Boy. To make the disguise perfect they had even extracted one of Westy Hogan's teeth on the right side of his mouth, and created a long scar on his left forefoot. No wonder they fooled Joe McLennan. Bookmakers in the United States were hit for a cool half-million in this sensational 'ringer' case. It made headlines around North America.

Staff Doyle, one of the owners, subsequently confessed to me during a Stanley Cup play-off in Detroit that he and his partners had cleaned up handsomely. "But you should not have held Westy Hogan" commented Doyle. "It cost us $60,000 to get him back." I have never been able to discover who received the $60,000, but I have my suspicions. I didn't receive one red cent of it.

Westy Hogan, aka Little Boy.

If the Westy Hogan ringer case was a major-league scam, Gorman's story about a former British officer from western Canada is more of a minor-league one. Nobody made much money on this one, but the haughty Major Kenyon did manage to eat for a few more days.

> *Someone informed me that the proud former officer had gone broke and he and his horses were without food. He indignantly refused a loan, but intimated he would dearly love to win a six-furlong dash with the pride and joy of his little stable. So we entered the horse, Princess Ethel, in a race and calculated that if the fellow could capture the purse he'd have enough to get home to the Rockies. There were some pretty fine men around the track at that time and we explained the circumstances. Well, to make it brief they agreed to give the British officer a break.*
>
> *But just at the last minute another entry slipped into the race, and this latest one refused to have anything to do with the proposed generosity towards the major's horse. There had to be some skullduggery. It was arranged that the two guards near the new owner's stable should disappear for an hour or so. We decided, in fact, they should be our guests for lunch.*
>
> *Well, the major's horse broke in front and was never headed. She won by a good length, and our gallant major cheered wildly and dashed to the winner's circle. His troubles were over for the time being.*
>
> *But mine were not! Ten minutes after the race the large figure of George Stein, the newly-arrived owner, blocked*

> *the sunlight in the door of my office. "Twenty years on the tracks" he shouted, "and that's the dirtiest trick yet." "Why George" I asked innocently, "what happened? You lose a bet?" "Yes!" he shouted. "What's more, somebody got into my stable and put lead shoes on my filly. No wonder she finished last!" Anyway, there was hay, oats and beefsteaks in the major's stable for a while. Opposing owners, incidentally, all kept their promises. They did not bet one dollar on the race.*

Politicians wouldn't normally fall under the heading of Gangsters, Gamblers and Ringers—but maybe some of them, at least, would qualify. The disastrous race meeting at Syracuse, New York in 1934 is a good example. Joe Cattarinich and Leo Dandurand, two Montreal sportsmen and top businessmen, were close acquaintances of Tay Pay. Cattarinich and Dandurand leased the Syracuse fairgrounds, brought in some top racing officials "and suddenly advised me that I had been appointed secretary."

> *Well and good, but where would we get the steeds? Leo explained that this was the problem of his partner Joe, and that as an Irish athlete I should not worry too much about it. True to his word, Joe Cattaranich supplied the thoroughbreds. Goodness knows where Joe had located them but there they were, and the race meeting started.*
>
> *Then legal troubles commenced to pile up. Injunctions, writs, summonses and Lord knows what followed in the wake of a New York political volcano. Every time I moved, someone handed me some type of a red-sealed legal document. There were bailiffs, sheriffs, process servers and State Troopers galore. Really, I began to*

hear handcuffs rattling in my sleep. In any event the race meeting got underway and people flocked to the Syracuse Fairgrounds. It looked like a grand success and Cattarinich and Dandurand had obviously scored another turf triumph.

Then came the crash. With the grandstand crowded and people fighting their way to the pari-mutuel machines State Troopers with loaded guns, motorcycles, horses and motor cars dramatically moved in. They closed the meeting after threatening to confiscate our $100,000 bankroll and threatening to arrest everyone involved.

Between the Democrats and Republicans, Leo and Joe had really been shaken down and forced to vamoose. Subsequently I asked Joe "I thought you really had everything tied up with those New York State politicians. What really happened?" A sheepish, apologetic grin came over his handsome countenance. "I have a frank confession to make to my Irish pal," replied Mr. Cattarinich. "We paid off the wrong guys!"

That was the last thoroughbred race meeting conducted in Syracuse.

Tommy's life around various racetracks inevitably brought him into contact with some characters of questionable repute. His memoirs include finding out that the real owner of the Mount Royal track in Montreal in the 1920s was none other than 'Lucky' Luciano, a notorious mob figure then under indictment in New York and subsequently exiled to Italy. TP discusses the sad end of Goat-Eye, a backstretch character at Toronto's Woodbine racetrack.

During the 1934 hockey season Goat-Eye rushed up to me at Maple Leaf Gardens, saying "I hold my lucky rabbit's foot every time your Black Hawks play. You cannot lose, with Goat-Eye in your corner." I told Goat-Eye that if the Black Hawks won the Stanley Cup I would send him a new suit, new hat and new shoes, plus shirts, neckties and pajamas. Well, Chicago carried off the Stanley Cup and we shipped along the promised wardrobe supplies. But poor old Goat-Eye wasn't a well-dressed gentleman for long. A week or two later they found him murdered near Woodbine. He was all dressed up in his new clothing which the Black Hawk players had sent. His lucky rabbit's foot had been stolen. Poor old Goat-Eye. He must have looked too prosperous.

Tommy tells this story about his hockey pal, big Bill Dwyer:

We were spinning along towards Belmont Park on a gorgeous autumn afternoon. Bill Dwyer had a $50,000 bet riding on one horse. "Hey Bill" asked Leo Rosenthal, "what is that fellow Harry who lived down that street doing now?" ... "Hard to say," answered Bill, "he has been dead for three years." Bill lost that bet without a tremor. One day the following week after a photo finish he turned and remarked "Now we can eat well tonight. I just won twenty grand on that gelding." He was one of the most unforgettable characters I have ever met."

Tommy loves to tell stories about newcomers to the racing game.

One morning Judge George Schilling discovered one of our new horse owners kicking and scraping the sand in front of the official stand. "What are you looking for, my good friend?" inquired Judge Schilling. "My jockey lost his battery," drawled the southerner. "Maybe it is around here somewhere." Exit another new owner. The stewards made him sell all his thoroughbreds and stick to the automobile business.

Then, as now, the supply of race horses could be a problem. But a problem is simply a solution waiting to be found, and Gorman and his people became adept at solving this particular problem.

During the war years when we were trying desperately to keep thoroughbred racing alive in Montreal, some most unusual customers appeared on the scene. It was so tough to secure horses that we rounded up $10,000 and sent one of our men to Cleveland and other tracks in Ohio to purchase some of the four-footed flyers. He made some good connections and soon horses began to arrive. The first meeting had to be postponed because we did not have enough horses to fill the cards and some of the owners became suspicious that we would not be able to open at all. One of them was a raggedy-looking trainer who landed in unexpectedly from New England with 10 gallopers. He made himself comfortable at the Mount Royal track and finally found his way up to my Windsor Hotel office.

"What is really behind this delay?" he inquired. "My idle horses are costing me $50 per day. If it is money you need, let me know." I explained that we needed horses, not money, but he proved a most persistent old racing enthusiast. "Look here" he said, "I have $10,000 you may have until the racing season ends." ... "How did you get

> *the $10,000?" I wanted to know, "and where is it now?" "Betting on the ponies in Florida," he explained, "and it's right here in my pocket, right next to my gun." We didn't take his 10 grand, but we did make him hand over that six-shooter. The next day he deposited $10,000 in the Royal Bank. Racing started the following Saturday and our strange pal had a banner summer. When he shipped out after the final meeting at Blue Bonnets he still had his $10,000 and his shooting iron. "*

Another year there was a problem finding enough horses for the Connaught Park meeting.

> *We had Harold Steinman's 'Roller Vanities' playing in the Auditorium at the time and one of his associates told me he knew a certain gentleman in New York who could send me several box-car loads of good thoroughbreds. He was then extremely powerful in many ways. So off to New York I trekked, holding a business card on which had been scribbled 'This guy is all right, a friend of mine.'*
>
> *I secured the appointment by telephone and drove up to a sumptuous apartment in Central Park West. There were three or four strange-looking people in the apartment although the lady who received me was really a knock-out. The boss had been out playing golf all day, she explained. He would be available shortly. She slipped out quietly when the 'Big Fellow,' now in immaculate evening clothes, made his appearance, waiving his two associates out of the finely furnished parlor. He spoke softly and asked how many I would require.*

> *"About 60" I replied. "That's a lot" he added "but if Joe sent you, you must be square. You go to the East River Bank at 10 o'clock tomorrow morning and it will be there in your name." Then it dawned on me: he thought I wanted 60G's, not 60 gee-gees. "I don't want money, I want horses "I explained, greatly embarrassed. "Well," he continued "that's even harder. How did you ever guess I had horses?" But he shipped me the 60 horses from Charlestown, West Virginia, and they saved the situation at Connaught Park.*
>
> *My handsome benefactor on that memorable occasion was none other than the now-famous Frank Erickson. Erickson was New York's largest bookmaker during the 1930s and '40s. He became well-known among bookmakers everywhere for handling 'lay-off' bets. His image was bashed by the media because of supposed connections with the mob, but these allegations were never proven.*

Probably no sport outside of horse racing has given birth to so many colorful nicknames, or such a splendid sense of humour, sometimes bizarre but always amusing. Tommy's memoirs include tales about Motion Picture Brown, "who was unfortunately pushed off the grandstand at Tanforan," Outlaw Olson, High Ball Kelly, Hand-ridin' Cloran, and Harry Sinclair of Standard Oil and Teapot Dome scandal fame, who "coolly dropped $20,000, at the roulette table in Agua Caliente, then kept the game going until he won it all back." There were some not-very-good steeplechase jockeys whose agent introduced them to Tommy as Banjo Hewitt, Hopeless Hudson and Fall Off Lefevre.

> *Next afternoon we started eight horses in the two-mile steeplechase and never in all my days have I seen anything like that aerial exhibition. At the first hurdle they nearly all flew into the air like men without flying trapezes. I thought Larry Sunbrock's rodeo had come to Connaught Park! After that sunny afternoon, we cancelled the 'jumps.'*

Gangsters, gamblers, ringers: they were all part of T.P.'s extraordinary life at the race track.

INSIDE THE SQUARED CIRCLE

For a sports promoter there were no better cities than Montreal and New York, and Tommy Gorman was up close and personal with those dynamic cities through much of his career. He loved the action, whatever it might be. Boxing and wrestling were among the events that caught his eye and while they were not the focus of his considerable energy they were a significant side-bar, bringing him into close contact with the famous names of that era who were responsible for filling Madison Square Garden and the Montreal Forum. He particularly enjoyed the New York fight fans.

> *Ten thousand fight fans were witnessing a 'waltz' in the Madison Square Garden prize ring. "Turn out the lights; they want to be alone!" boomed a voice from the Upper Circle. "No, don't turn out the lights "shouted a man who had paid $25 for his ringside seat. "I want to read my newspaper."*

T.P. enjoyed the New York fight mob too.

> *One cannot forget the handsomely dressed second who thrust his head through the ropes and shouted as his fighter was being battered to pieces: "Stay in there and slug. He can't hurt us!"*

Then there was the time one of his acquaintances convinced Gorman to give his new fighter, perhaps the Great White Hope, a chance in the Garden ring.

> *In the opening round of his first Garden battle he was up and down eight or nine times before they stopped the fight. The New York Tribune referred to him as 'The Human Elevator.' I came across him about a year later on Broadway. "I'm making progress" he declared. "I have been knocked out in nine of my last 10 fights but as they say, there is no substitute for experience."*

Tommy's interest in boxing might well have been kindled in 1926, the year of the great Jack Dempsey-Gene Tunney fight in Philadelphia. Gorman and his good friend John Bain, drove to New York where they caught the Champagne Special[30] to Philly to see the big fight.

> *What a real escapade that turned out to be. Liquor flowed like water, there were cabaret performances in the aisles, and half-clad dancers flitted in and out of the Pullmans. To Mr. Bain this must have been quite a revelation.*

> *The fight was an outdoor affair in front of more than 120,000 boxing fans, a record at the time. The heavens broke wide open during the latter stages of the*

30 A Pennsylvania Railroad train scheduled specifically for bringing well-heeled fans from New York to the bout.

heavyweight fight and every time Tunney hit Dempsey blood shot up toward the ring lights. Jack was literally cut to pieces and Gene gained the decision. John and I became separated after the battle, with tens of thousands milling around looking for taxis and buses. We managed to rejoin one another at the Broad Street station, after which we climbed back aboard the Champagne Special.

And the show they had presented between New York and Philadelphia was nothing compared to what took place on the return journey. It was really terrific. The sky proved the limit. I recall everyone had become soaking wet, and some of the show gals just threw their dresses into heaps on the seats and sat carelessly in their undies. There were wrestling matches, boxing battles, gambling for big stakes with crap games all over the train.

Gorman and Bain were invited to a continuation of the celebration when the Champagne Special pulled into New York. Bain opted for the comfort of his hotel room after such a riotous day and evening. Gorman went to the party.

A dozen years later it was wrestling which attracted Gorman's eye. Not without initial opposition from some directors of The Canadian Arena Company for whom Gorman worked, though. Some looked askance at the business, finding it just a little unsavory. But Gorman's logic prevailed, and he brought forth a man who would become one of the great names in wrestling in that era, Yvon Robert.

Robert won the world championship in Boston in front of 15,000 fans, and then made his debut at The Forum before a sold-out crowd a short time later. And what an attraction he proved to be. Robert, a dashing

French-Canadian performing in front of his adoring fans, filled buildings in Montreal, Ottawa, Quebec, Chicoutimi, Sherbrooke, and wherever he went. He has been a veritable mint for the Forum owners, and those directors who originally opposed the return of wrestling soon changed their minds. Many still criticize the 'grunt and groan' artists, but they never fail to provide spectacular entertainment. Grapplers, in the opinion of many, are the best trained and best disciplined athletes in the world. The smartest, the best educated and the finest-disciplined athletes I have ever associated with were members of the much-maligned wrestling fraternity.

FIRST-CLASS, RIGHT TO THE END

On a January night in 1961, hundreds gathered at the stately Chateau Laurier Hotel in Ottawa for the annual Associated Commercial Travelers Sportsman's' Dinner. The event always attracted a sell-out crowd and some of the biggest names in sport lent their speaking skills to this, one of the most important events on the Ottawa calendar.

This night, the podium was shared by several outstanding personalities from the world of sport. Jersey Joe Walcott was there, one of the greatest boxers ever. Mel Allen was there, the unforgettable Voice of the Yankees. Charlie Dressen was there, the manager of the Milwaukee Braves. So was Ronnie Stewart, the great running back of the Ottawa Rough Riders.

T.P. was there too, dressed resplendently in a tuxedo and as most in the room would come to realize, this was his final public appearance. His speech was terrific, according to newspaper reports and if his voice itself was a little crackly thanks to his ongoing health issue, there was nothing wrong with his mind, and his great sense of humour. He regaled his large audience with several wonderful stories, and he was rewarded with a lengthy standing ovation.

Less than four months later, on May 15, 1961, Thomas Patrick Gorman died.

Newspapers across Canada and in several U.S. cities carried lengthy obituaries, and his death brought a slew of telegrams and letters to the Gorman residence on Clemow Avenue where his wake was held. There was a mountain of flowers sent from across North America, and hundreds turned out for his funeral from Blessed Sacrament Church just a few blocks from his home, including many from the hockey and entertainment worlds where he had cut such a wide swath. Among the many tributes which arrived is one that stands out. It is a handwritten letter to Tommy's son Frank, written on House of Commons letterhead, fitting, perhaps, because that is where T.P.'s extraordinary working life had begun, some 66 years earlier:

> *Dear Frank:*
>
> *I was saddened and shocked by your father's death. Please accept—for all members of the family—my deep and sincere sympathy. I have been thinking of you all, and especially of your mother, at this sad time.*
>
> *What a wonderful person he was, dynamic, full of life and imagination and with a zest to do things. The sporting and athletic life of a nation is important—very important—and your father made a great contribution to this side of Canada's development.*
>
> *I shall always remember with great pleasure my own contacts with him. He was always so warm and friendly. God rest his generous soul.*
>
> *As ever,*
> *Mike Pearson.*

Mike Pearson was, of course, the Honourable Lester B. Pearson, Prime Minister of Canada from 1963 to 1968. Pearson had won a Nobel Peace Prize in 1957, and was the Leader of the Opposition at the time he wrote to Frank.

It was perhaps fitting that Tommy Gorman's funeral mass be something out of the ordinary. It had all the bells and whistles and was celebrated by his cousin, Bishop Thomas K. Gorman, the Bishop of Dallas-Fort Worth, Texas. The Bishop made sure his cousin had one, last, first-class ride because as T.P. had said so often: "Always go first class!"

He did, from beginning to end.

MUCH MORE THAN A FOOTNOTE

Bishop Thomas Kiely Gorman deserves much more than a footnote. His long life was full of travel and accomplishment, worthy of much closer study than is afforded here. He was a first cousin of T.P. and the two kept in close touch over the years. Bishop Tom, or just The Bishop as most in the family called him, was born in Pasadena, California, in 1892. He was the son of James Gorman, who shortly before had left the Gorman's Prince Edward Island home for the far west.

He had a remarkably long and successful career in the Catholic Church. Ordained to the priesthood in 1917, he served under eight popes. He was a world traveler, studying in Belgium and attending the Second Vatican Council in Rome, Italy in the 1960s. He became a close friend of Bishop Fulton J. Sheen, the 'TV Bishop' who he met while studying in Belgium.

Printers' ink ran through his veins, as it did through so many Gorman veins, and he loved the newspaper world. He was editor and publisher of *The Tidings* in the Los Angeles Diocese, founded *The Nevada Register*, re-established *The Texas Catholic* and developed the National Catholic News Service.

By April, 1931, he had been appointed the first Bishop of the Diocese of Reno, Nevada, which encompassed the entire state. In 1952 Pope Pius XII appointed him as coadjutor bishop in Dallas-Fort Worth, Texas. Two years later he was named Bishop there, remaining for 15 years until his retirement in 1969. Among his many accomplishments were the establishment of the University of Dallas, and the building of five new high schools and several new hospitals in the area. "If ever there was any Bishop loved by his fellow Bishops it was he," Bishop Sheen said at an event honoring his old classmate.

The Bishop died in 1980 at the age of 87 and is buried in Dallas.

Bishop T.K. Gorman.

A REPORTER'S REPORTER

One of the most revered and respected sports writers in Canada was Bill Westwick, uncle of Tommy's wife Mary (Mae), she being a sister of Harry 'Rat' Westwick of Silver Seven fame. Bill Westwick would himself be worthy of a special book and certainly deserves a mention in this one.

Westwick worked for T.P. at Connaught Park for many years as a thoroughbred steward and standardbred judge. As a reporter and sports columnist he covered many of Gorman's adventures during his own brilliant career.

Westwick was the Sports Editor of *The Ottawa Journal* from 1942 until his retirement in 1973, and there were few major events in the sporting world which he did not cover. As his obituary in the *Ottawa Citizen* noted, he covered The Maurice Richard Riot of 1955, Don Larsen's perfect game in 1956, Bill Mazeroski's World Series-winning home run in 1960, Cassius Clay winning the World Heavyweight Championship in 1964 and so many other momentous sporting occasions. At his retirement he was awarded the keys to the City of Ottawa. Bill won a number of awards for writing. He was inducted into the Canadian Football League Hall of Fame (Media Division) and also into the Ottawa Sports Hall of Fame.

He and Tommy made a memorable automobile trip together to the west coast to visit some of Tommy's old haunts, and then on to Texas to pay a visit to The Bishop. Some small portions of that excursion found their way into Bill's columns but reading between the lines, it must have been quite the escapade.

Bill died in 1990, remembered by so many friends as a good reporter, a man of uncommon decency and a man who built a tremendous level of trust amongst the people he worked with. He was a reporter's reporter.

In short, a great guy to have as a relative. Perhaps someone will pull together the best of Bill's thousands of columns. They would tell quite a story about the major sporting events which helped to shape North America in the thirty-plus years he was Sports Editor of *The Ottawa Journal.*

CHRONOLOGY OF T.P. GORMAN

1886	Born on June 9, 1886, in Ottawa, Ontario
1895	Served as Page Boy, House of Commons, Ottawa
1908	Won Gold Medal with Canadian Olympic Lacrosse Team, London, England
1910	Married Mary Elizabeth Westwick
1912	Named Sports Editor, Ottawa Citizen
1917	Joined Ottawa Senators Hockey Club as Manager.
1917	Participated in the formation of The National Hockey League
1919	Joined Connaught Park Jockey Club as Secretary
1920	Won his first Stanley Cup, as manager of the Ottawa Senators
1921	Won his second Stanley Cup, as manager of the Ottawa Senators
1923	Won his third Stanley Cup, as manager of the Ottawa Senators
1925	Sold interest in Ottawa Senators, helped form New York Americans in NHL
1928	Withdrew from hockey to devote time to horse racing in Agua Caliente, Mexico, Ottawa and Montreal
1933	Returned to NHL as manager of the Chicago Black Hawks

1934	Won his fourth Stanley Cup, as coach and manager of the Chicago Black Hawks
1934	Left Chicago to become manager of the Montreal Maroons (NHL) and manager of the Montreal Forum
1935	Won his fifth Stanley Cup, as coach and manager of the Montreal Maroons
1942	Became manager of the Montreal Canadiens after Maroons withdrew from the NHL
1944	Won his sixth Stanley Cup, as manager of the Montreal Canadiens
1946	Won his seventh Stanley Cup, as manager of the Montreal Canadiens
1946	Left Montreal to take over the Ottawa Auditorium, the Ottawa Senators (QSHL) and Connaught Park Jockey Club
1948	Brought pro baseball back to Ottawa, as owner of the Ottawa Nationals. Won the Border League championship three of the next four years
1949	Won the Allan Cup, as owner of the Ottawa Senators
1950	Took Barbara Ann Scott on coast-to-coast tour
1953	Conducted first night thoroughbred racing in Canada, at Connaught Park
1954	Promoted night harness racing at Connaught Park
1954	Withdrew the Ottawa Senators from the Quebec Hockey league
1955	Sold the Ottawa Auditorium to concentrate on horse racing at Connaught Park
1961	Died on May 15, 1961, in Ottawa, Ontario
1963	Elected to the Hockey Hall of Fame
1966	Elected to the Ottawa Sport Hall of Fame
1973	Elected to the Canadian Horse Racing Hall of Fame

A proud T.P. with wife Mae and children Joe, Betty and Frank, c. 1945.

www.ingramcontent.com/pod-product-compliance
Ingram Content Group UK Ltd.
Pitfield, Milton Keynes, MK11 3LW, UK
UKHW040604210726
13854UKWH00009B/2555